I Want To Retire!

Essential Considerations

For the Retiree to Be

By Dave Bernard

Copyright 2013

Dedicated to my wife and our retirement
to be

*****

Happy is the man who finds a true
friend,

And far happier is he who finds that
true friend in his wife.

~ Franz Schubert

Table of Contents

The biggest retirement surprise for me was how little time I have and how busy I seem to be every minute of every day. I don't know how I found the time to have a job! Also, that it I want to keep busy and occupied, I have to take the initiative and make plans and organize activities myself. Lastly, how scary it is to have to make major decisions by myself and to worry about what I will do as I get older and less able to be independent.

I want to retire! I am done with this career thing and more than ready to take a look at what life has to offer beyond work. It has been a good run but enough is enough and I need to get out while I am still young enough to enjoy my second act. I am ready to commence doing what I really want to do for as long as I choose to do it. I hope that retirement will be my moment to focus on what I am most passionate about, what inspires me, what excites me, what turns me on, and what makes me want to jump out of bed to start the day. It will also be my time to step back from the hectic and try my hand at a more peaceful relaxing existence. I am so ready to retire.

Many of us have likely entertained similar thoughts. And if you are middle age or beyond it is even possible your focus borders on the obsessive. Does the possibility of freedom to pursue your personal passions and pleasures tempt you to your very core? Do you find yourself expectantly hoping for that day when you will finally retire from the working world to your own personal nirvana? If you have been caught up in your career with its many demands over these many years, the dream of escaping to retirement may be the single most important thing that kept you going through the hard times.

The good news is if you can commit yourself to doing the ever important planning and preparation for the retirement life you want to live, there is no reason you – Mr. or Ms. Retiree to Be – should not be able to experience just that scenario. But if you want to arrive on schedule ready to roll, it is never too early to begin your preparations.

The ideal and very personal retirement life we ultimately live will be different for each of us. There is no cookie-cutter one-size-fits-all model guaranteed to lead us to and guide us through a fulfilling retirement. Each of us is driven by different motivations and our own distinct personal passions. A wide range of variables and life experiences have combined over the course of our lives to make us into the being that we are, for better or worse. And because of those variations we face the reality that though we may seek a common goal of living a happy retired life, the final definition of that happiness can differ from person to person. My retirement Shangri la may be nothing like the vision of your perfect post-work paradise. Likewise, what I need to do to realize my personal retirement bliss may be nowhere near what you require to achieve the same. There is no absolute right or wrong way to live retirement. In the end we need to each discover those essential ingredients that will make up our personal fulfilling retirement and plot a course to navigate successfully to its shore.

How many of us have given any meaningful thought to our pending retirement? Beyond some vague concept of a life after work we don't tend to overly concern ourselves with the details. Until recently, I had not honestly contemplated my exit from the working world beyond occasionally imagining myself sitting on a sunny beach, cocktail in hand while I listen to the calming waves, reveling in my new freedom and the knowledge that there was absolutely nothing I had to be doing. And isn't that the way many think of retirement? Don't we typically view our second act as more of an escape from rather than a journey to?

I think that many of us assume that somehow it will all work out only to discover we are wrong. You need to prepare for retirement just as you do any other major step in your life. Just like the reluctant retiree, we have to learn on the job if you will. I think it is important to be open to the possibilities rather than focusing on the limitations. You do have some choices if you keep your mind open.

For most of us the tremendous demands of daily life from bill paying to family raising, from problem solving to nest egg building suck up all our energy. It is not too surprising that the focus remains on here and now rather than what our future may hold. Yet if we let life continue to pass us by without taking the necessary steps to prepare, if we expect to just suddenly arrive in retirement where everything will take care of itself, we may find ourselves sadly mistaken.

How many of us can honestly say that we have taken steps to plan and prepare for retirement? What have we done to understand and address the many variables that will mix and match into that life we will realize beyond work? I would venture to say that most of us think of retirement as off in the distance, somewhere down the road, nothing to worry about right now. We are still young and have time – retirement is for old people. But have you looked in the mirror recently? The clock keeps ticking and before we know it we are looking back on more years than we foresee going forward. For those who will retire at age sixty five, retirement can extend twenty or thirty years. If we hope to fill those years with a meaningful and fulfilling life the sooner we start preparing ourselves the better. In my own case I realized that outside of regularly contributing to my 401k plan I had made no concrete preparation for retirement. I was just as guilty as anyone of not looking ahead. I was just as guilty of not preparing myself for the retiree I would be. And if I continued down this path, I risk potentially ending up in just as much trouble as others who follow a similar course.

My advice is to plan, plan, plan for everything, and then realize you have no idea what is going to happen and that is OK. Plans are meant to evolve, be discarded, and replaced with other plans. Your retirement will be like a blank canvas. You'll buy all the paints and brushes but will have no idea what it will look like until you start applying the paint.

Some years ago I found time to pause from my hectic life due to a change in employment status (otherwise known as no more job). In retrospect it turned out to be a blessing as I was afforded the opportunity to re-evaluate my life and examine the direction in which I was headed. At age fifty two I was no longer a young buck and retirement was no longer just a distant possibility but rather an ever-more-rapidly-approaching eventuality. Sixty five is a lot closer to fifty two than to twenty two. So, in addition to merely analyzing my career past, present and future I decided to take advantage of my momentary job pause and go one step further. Assuming that I would in fact retire at some point in the future, this hiatus was my opportunity to begin researching and learning what I could do to better prepare myself for retirement.

What can I do between now and when I retire to make sure I experience a first rate, not to be

*outdone, every day a new inspiration, just plain
awesome retirement life?*

*How can I improve my odds of finding that retired
life just right for me?*

*What are the most important areas I need to
consider and prepare for?*

What are the most common pitfalls to avoid?

What realities can I expect to encounter?

As good a place as any to start, I went to Google
and did a search on "retirement". You would be
surprised – or maybe not so much – with the
incredibly vast and quickly overwhelming number
of websites and blogs and articles and studies you
can find just searching for that single word (My
search came up with 225,000,000 hits).

I discovered an incredible amount of attention
given to financial preparation for retirement.
Hundreds and thousands of blogs, magazines,
articles, reviews, and news sites were dedicated to
helping prepare financially for the retired life you
eventually hope to live. Everything you could ever
want to know about investing for retirement was
covered and covered again…and again. Financial
experts and investment magazines, stock brokers
and fund managers, bloggers and authors all
shared their views, predictions and
recommendations. And with an epic aging baby

boomer population, this is an incredibly important piece in the overall retirement planning puzzle. Without enough money you can only dream of living a fulfilling retirement. Despite all of this shared knowledge it is a sad current state of affairs with regards to financial preparedness for retirement. According to the Employee Benefit Research Institute 46 percent of all American workers have less than $10,000 saved for retirement with 29 percent having less than $1000 saved.(1)

It appears that most retirees to be still have a long way to go to achieve the financial security portion of their retirement planning. The good news is there is a plethora of valuable information at our fingertips we just need to wade through it. And since I am no expert in things financial I will defer to this knowledge base for specifics about planning for retirement from a financial perspective.

However, there was another area of planning for retirement that I did not find nearly so well addressed. I believe there is a flip side to the retirement coin equally as important to successful retirement preparedness as financial planning. Once I have the money I need to retire, what do I actually do with my new found freedom and bushels of available time? How do I stay engaged and active to really make the most of my second act? I read too many stories and have met too many people who are bored, frustrated, unfulfilled and depressed about living their retirement life. Rather than viewed as a new chapter and the beginning of new adventures to be, they find retirement to be a letdown, a sad ending to what was previously an active life.

I want to do all I can ahead of time to avoid such an occurrence in my life. I want to figure out what I need to do to eventually live as close as possible to that vision of my perfect retirement dream.

During retirement we get the opportunity to do what we want to do. But we'd darn well better figure out what it is we want to do. For if we don't, we run the danger of waking up in the morning and sort of drifting our way through the day...then the next day, then the next. Yep, it may well take some time to find our "true retired self," but it's important that we do it, for then our retirement becomes rewarding.

To better understand this lesser known but equally important side of the retirement coin, I immersed myself in the world of retirement writers, authors, bloggers, experts, and those as interested as me in figuring out the retirement game. I quickly found one of the best sources of creative thinking to be numerous bloggers sharing their first hand experiences as they personally struggled to navigate the retirement jungle. Their discussions of what worked and what did not work, their fears and how they were coping, their detailed accounts of how they faced the realities of getting older and their real experiences of living the life of a retiree helped to clarify for me what we would all have to deal with at some point. I started to get a better feeling for what was required and what was in store and even some hints on how to more effectively get to that desired retirement life.

To best compile and share the results of my on-going education, in 2010 I launched my blog _Retirement – Only the Beginning._ The premise was and remains sharing information, insights, feedback and recommendations on how to best plan and prepare for a fulfilling retirement from a non-financial perspective. Just as we are coached to build our financial portfolio so, too, should we endeavor to build our non-financial portfolio consisting of guidelines and tools to live a worthwhile and inspired retired life.

We each need to learn how to effectively navigate the retirement jungle if we want to experience our own first class retirement life. Although one scenario of the perfect retirement may differ from another, there are some common threads. We may benefit from the experiences of others to help in our own journey. We can learn from other's mistakes so as to avoid repeating history. We can try to take steps now to prepare for tomorrow. It can be a mistake to take a seat along the sidelines and wait for retirement to happen.

But if we step up and take responsibility for our individual destiny, if we work at it and do the right things ahead of time, why should we not hope for an excellent retirement?

I Want To Retire! does not have answers for all of the complexities of preparing for a fulfilling and rewarding retirement. Rather, the focus is on bringing to light key areas to consider as you make your retirement plans. The reality is that we each will travel our own path to discover that retirement most ideal for our individual personality and situation. I can no more tell you how to experience yours than you can tell me how to find mine. But there are common themes and some specific topics to address that may help each of us realize that perfect second act.

To assist in our journey I share some insightful, honest, often passionate and always candid thoughts expressed in the more than 2000 comments readers of my retirement blogs have shared over the years. These comments are from a mix of retirees to be as well as those currently living retired life. Some are happy with where they are, some are confused, some are angry and many are still searching for the best way to live a fulfilling retirement. But one and all call it like they see it, adding firsthand experience along with a dose of reality to the topics discussed. And all have either sought or are seeking answers to the same questions will we all need to ask.

I invite you to read through the chapters and ask yourself how the information contained can best apply to your efforts to prepare for your second act. Take your time to peruse and contemplate these most essential considerations for successful retirement preparation.

I believe that each of us has a unique fulfilling retirement waiting to be discovered. We are different people with our own set of passions, beliefs, wishes and needs. In the end realizing our individual potential will require different things of each of us. There is really no single set of guidelines to direct one and all.

But we can improve our odds of getting to where we want to be if we try to focus on some important areas of retirement planning. We cannot cover nor plan for every minute detail but if we identify and contemplate those most essential considerations we can be off to a good start. We all want to hit our retirement life out of the park but to do so we need to keep our eye on the ball.

As the tag line for my blog reads "Retirement - Only the Beginning."

Shall we get started?

Chapter 1 - Redefining the Retired You

*The greatest danger is not that we aim too high
and miss it, but that we aim too low and reach it.*
~ Michelangelo

Having spent the majority of your life immersed in a career or possibly multiple careers, it should not be surprising that who you are and how you present yourself to the world has been greatly influenced by your work environment. Over the years you have learned how to engage and compete and succeed in what can be a rather hostile, highly competitive environment. You have honed skills and learned appropriate responses while developing a thick skin and the ability to act quickly on your feet. They say success in the corporate world can be a matter of survival of the fittest and over a life-long exposure you have learned what is required to succeed and flourish. Whether you remain one of the worker bees or have moved into the ranks of management, you have done your job well - kudos to you.

Now at the end of your career you find yourself at the doorway to what can be your life's next great adventure. As a retiree to be, you have earned the right to move into retirement where you hope to realize the promise of living the life you have always wanted, of doing the things you want rather than have to, of exploring new avenues and pursuing what you are truly passionate about. If you have been planning and preparing for this day you likely feel ready to make the move, heck you are probably anxious to do so! Let's get to it, daylight is burning. But just how ready are you really?

Boomers need to consider "what now?" before they retire. What will you do all day? We need to consider retirement hobbies, part time work or starting a small business, and simply finding new friends. Boomers need to consider their options. There are many retirement adventures left for you, just consider what you want your retirement to be and Go for It! P.S. If you are anxious over retirement, I'd bet you aren't ready. When you are really ready, you will know it without a doubt.

Remember that successful corporate warrior that you have so painstakingly evolved into over the past thirty years? Well when you leave the business arena and enter into the retired world a whole different skill set is needed. Those survival instincts that made you an A-player on the job do not necessarily transfer effectively into life outside of work. Your successful career-driven persona is generally not the best vehicle in which to realize a fulfilling retirement. As a matter of fact those behaviors that made you such a success can tend to be just plain out of place in your post-employment world. For example, you might mistakenly think that those negotiation tricks, those subtle ways to move someone toward the end result you desire can be employed to 'improve' the way your wife currently runs things around the house. Perhaps a worthwhile goal but you will need more than your business acumen alone to succeed in this new world.

And say goodbye to the power you wielded due to your exalted position in the corporate hierarchy. That goes right out the window the day you leave the company and become one of the retired masses. You may find yourself swapping your CEO moniker for the now more appropriate Citizen Entering Obscurity. How disheartening it must be to speak with someone at a party only to hear those painful words "Didn't you used to be...?" Redefining yourself in retirement is in many ways starting from scratch. How quickly and effectively you adapt can greatly impact how fulfilling a retirement you will experience.

As you leave the working you behind and take those first steps as a retiree, it is helpful to understand and develop who you want to be moving forward. It is important to separate the working you from the retired you. Now is your chance to make those adjustments that can improve upon who you are and move you to who you want to be in retirement.

Although we might think we know ourselves very well, the business of 9 to 5 has kept us from probing into understanding who we really are and what we really want from life.

This adjustment applies as well to the at-home spouse who has been responsible for maintaining the home, raising the kids and holding it all together along the way. After years of selfless commitment to the needs of others, the promise of retirement is just as sweet and just as tantalizing. Realizing dreams of doing what they want is just as important to their sanity. And in an interesting turn of events it can be the case that the at-home spouse is actually better prepared for the monumental changes retirement will introduce. In many cases, this person has already had to deal with a major change when it came time for the children to move on. Suddenly the days were no longer packed with to-do lists and commitments of the kids. With this newly realized freedom, it became important to find other interests and activities. And so this spouse has already begun to reach outside of the life they lived to broaden their horizons and engage them self. They have had the time to establish friendships, research interesting organizations, explore new hobbies, and generally occupy themselves as an independent individual. They have effectively gone through many of those exercises that their partner will soon need to explore.

What can we do to help in this transition from the working person we used to be to the retired person we want to be? How can we get there with the least difficulty and greatest likelihood of success?

Be easy on yourself

There is real value in planning ahead so that you can better predict what your retirement will look like. But as you start your retirement life, don't be too hard on yourself. Realize that this retirement thing is new to you. You have no prior experience and will have to feel your way through it all as the day's progress. Fortunately there is no schedule to follow and no guidelines you must adhere to. You get to set your own pace and try different things. There is in fact nothing that you have to do or should be doing or cannot do if you so choose. Don't get overanxious if the road ahead is not crystal clear. Cut yourself some slack and just go with the flow.

You may feel under pressure to get productive the minute you retire. You fear wasting valuable time and so might feel a bit antsy about getting started on something worthwhile. Rather than gradually progressing into your retirement life you might feel the need to jump at suggestions of others, things like volunteering, traveling the world, maybe even planning an encore career. The ink on your exit papers is hardly dry and you are already trying to fill your day. You have not even given yourself time to figure out what it is that you really want to be doing. Don't make the mistake of jumping prematurely into something just to be busy. You don't want to find yourself engaged in an activity that you really would prefer not to be doing. Feel free to waste some time. Realize that time you enjoy wasting is not really wasted, is it?

One of my blog readers offers some good advice: *Be easy on yourself when you first retire. You may struggle with feelings of guilt for not being productive, or feel in a hurry to get involved in a volunteer opportunity or other structure. I think it's best to ease into it and just enjoy the freedom. Just let it take you where it leads instead of forcing it to be like you may have pictured. Easier said than done, I know.*

Take your time to better understand the lay of the land. Be willing to try different things. Don't feel you have to be living one particular way or doing some particular things. Get rid of any guilt you may be feeling for not being productive – you don't have to be productive all the time. Take it easy on yourself during the early retired days realizing you have many years ahead.

You start with a clean slate

During your career your hard work and extra efforts hopefully led to recognition for a job well done. Perhaps you proudly displayed awards on your walls celebrating hard-earned successes while your business card reflected the important person you were. Now in retirement you may find it beneficial to begin to shift away from the person you were. Those corporate victories do not readily translate into the life of a retiree. What was such a source of pride when shared in the company setting can carry little or no weight now. How sad it is to encounter an ex-CEO whose powerful position and far reaching influence no longer holds any real significance. How much sadder when that same CEO retires yet still behaves as if he had that supreme control, puffing out his chest and ordering others around. No one now has to abide by his commands and all his huffing and puffing are no more than hot air quickly dissipating along with his misplaced feelings of self-importance. Such an individual needs to realize what was then and what is now and learn to evolve into a new role in retirement.

Consider in retirement you are starting from scratch. Although what you did during your working life may be interesting, who you are in retirement will be more based on what you do as a member of the retired. Don't expect to lean on your work accomplishments as your stories may quickly bore those around you. What you do with your life from this point forward is what will impact how you are perceived by those around you.

This time of change can be a wonderful opportunity. No matter who you were in your past life you now have a chance to become who you want to be. Those annoying habits that drove others to distraction can be whittled away like so much dead wood. You have the opportunity to reinvent yourself into the person you want to be. The slate is clean and you are holding the chalk.

Try not to waste this second chance. Ask yourself what specifically others do that most annoys you.

Then take a close look at yourself and ask if you share any of those same characteristics. Ask yourself if there are areas in which you would like to personally improve. Remember how you learned to set and pursue goals while working? Here is your opportunity to utilize those same skills and set new goals for the retired you.

You can remake a new you
When someone you meet asks what it is you do, how do you describe yourself? While a member of the work force the accepted and expected response is along the lines of what you do on your job. I am a sales manager for a start-up or I am VP of Marketing for such-and-such company or I write code for apps. Who we are and how we define ourselves is intimately tied to our particular career. And this makes perfect sense as we spend more time on the job than in any other life pursuit.

But as a retiree who will no longer have a regular job, how will you describe yourself? How would you **like** to describe yourself? Is there a new identity that you might like to assume? A good first step in the process of redefining the new you is to realize who you were on the job is no longer who you are. The sum total of personality traits and acquired skills that made up your work persona may have been well-suited for you on the job. But that was then. In retirement you have a chance to establish a new you, to redefine who you will be from this point on.

How do you view yourself today and how would you like to see yourself in the future? Here are a few questions to help dig in a bit to understand you.

Who are you now?

What is it about you personally that sets you apart from others?

Are you generally optimistic or pessimistic?

What single thing about you do you hope a new acquaintance will walk away with after your first meeting?

Describe yourself to you.

What areas interest you and excite you?

What is it about you that makes you loveable?

How would your best friend describe the person you are?

What things do you want to accomplish?

What dreams do you have?

What makes you laugh or cry?

Who and what do you hold most dear?

What one thing would be hardest for you to sacrifice?

What traits in others do you most admire?

Who is your hero?

What about you would a child most admire?

What would you do if you were not afraid?

We are no longer constrained to be that person we were on the job. We are much more. Outside of the job we have interests and passions that hint toward the real person we are. We have strong feelings that influence our actions and stimulate our intellect. We feel pride, respect, honor, elation, sorrow and fear outside of anything to do with work. Although a significant influence, our job ultimately defines only a part of who we are.

Going from a full time job to no job may seem ideal, but it is an enormous and difficult adjustment. Too many retired people end up feeling useless, with no purpose. Many suffer from episodic depression as a result, making what could be the best time of their lives, the worst time. Prepare yourself by finding a passion to pursue during retirement.

So I am at a get together sipping a nice Pinot Noir when someone I do not know sidles up next to me. We nod a brief hello and I know it is just a matter of time before I will be asked "what do you do?" Although I am not working at any specific job that does not mean I have nothing to say. I am a father of two awesome children with whom I have been blessed to grow up alongside over the past years. I am husband to the most amazing lady whose humor and heartfelt love sustains me and inspires me each day. I am a lover of music and rarely does a day pass where some song does not bring on a tear or a laugh or a warm memory. I believe in God and do my best to always treat others the way I hope they would treat me. I love little kids especially for short periods of time. Robin Williams still makes me laugh like a madman. I find strength and comfort in the sound of the waves breaking against the shore and will never grow tired of the incredible beauty of each new sunset. Sappy movies can make me cry. The perfect verse or poem strikes me to my core. I can be too quick to react before thinking something through, have been known to speak too fast when I am excited, on occasion hug someone for no apparent reason, and tend to wear a smile even when I sleep (as witnessed in the permanent smile lines). I am more than my work, far more. And I am just beginning.

In our new role as retirees we will have time to reflect and better understand which on-the-job personality traits will fit in with and compliment our future. We also have the opportunity to prune as necessary those traits with no place in our retirement life.

You are able redefine success

One of the nice things about a career in sales is there are clear well defined measures of success. If you achieve your sales quota you are successful. And if you do not you have failed. Clear cut, no room for misinterpretation, it is what it is. I have always found it somewhat comforting that at any given time, based upon progress toward my goals, I can tell if I am doing a good job and earning my keep. Basically, I can tell whether I am successful or not.

As a retiree, we will enter a new chapter in life. And in this new chapter there tends to be far less clear cut measures of success. If you are someone who functions best when you have goals to pursue with measures of progress along the way you might find retirement a bit challenging. Now things are not based on dollars and cents. Project deadlines no longer loom in your immediate future. With your new found freedom to do what you want, how will you know if you are successful? What really is success in retirement?

Retirement is different for everyone. Some like to travel, some like to work part-time and some enjoy just being a part of their grandchildren's lives.

Success in retirement living can be different things to different people. Some will still have the need to define a target outcome and then work toward its completion. You witness this behavior in the perpetual project doer who goes from building a new deck to re-landscaping the backyard to modifying the car engine and on and on. Success and satisfaction come from getting the job done and done well. Then move on to the next project.

Others may measure success in a less concrete way. Some can find satisfaction in helping others to navigate their life path. For others success can be found in making small improvements to the person they are, perhaps breaking a bad habit or taking up a new good behavior. Still others can realize a measure of success by taking the time to look inside themselves to better understand the real person they are.

Success can be something uniquely molded to fit each of us. The good news is we get to define for ourselves exactly what it is. We do not have to measure it in terms of dollars or awards or recognition. We set our own goals for achievement in retirement. And should we decide that we need no hard and fast measures of success that is just fine too.

You can keep learning

My advice to someone heading into retirement is to have so many fun things going that you cannot wait to get going down that road. Be sure to do those things in your daily routine that keep you healthy physically, emotionally and spiritually. Life is good and retirement is great.

You can't teach an old dog new tricks, or can you? Not that we should necessarily view ourselves as old dogs just because we are heading toward retirement! But are we too old to learn? Do we still have the capacity and the curiosity to be interested in learning new things? Realistically is there anything that we do not already know after having traipsed through 65 years of life on this planet?

Henry Ford said, *"Anyone who stops learning is old whether at twenty or eighty. Anyone who keeps learning stays young. The greatest thing in life is to keep your mind young."*

There is always more to learn and in retirement we will have the freedom to look beyond what we are required to learn and begin to investigate what we actually want to learn. Without the pressure of grades or graduating we now have the luxury to study those subjects that genuinely interest us. In the bygone days of school we may have had to forego those creative art and music classes as our days were already filled with core subjects like math and science and English. Happily that is no longer the case as we bask in our newly discovered freedom of choice. Should you find yourself in search of stimulating undertakings to keep you engaged in retired life taking classes might be just the ticket. And not only can taking classes improve our mind and capture our interest it also gets us out of the house and allows us to interact with others. We have the chance to discover what our neighborhood has to offer and best of all try something new.

Our quest for knowledge and our natural curiosity do not end or necessarily even diminish as we age. There is always something new that catches out interest or has us searching for additional information. I cannot watch a National Geographic show without being driven to the web to search for additional specifics on the one of a kind reptile found only in one part of the world that is the subject of their documentary. When we watch a show that is filmed on location you can bet my wife and I pull out the atlas to see exactly where that location is in relation to our own little piece of the world. We are all curious about different things and that curiosity can provide an incentive to learn more.

Lifelong learning is a natural for senior citizens. We have time available. We get to pick those topics that most interest us. Learning requires that we use our brains which helps keep us sharp and makes our conversations worthy of attention. And learning can help to keep us socially engaged with others.

You may want to broaden your network of friends

Friends and acquaintances established while working find common ground in the shared work effort and business environment. You come to know one another over the course of months and years as you unite to make the company successful. And during that time you on occasion build friendships.

Once work is left behind you may suddenly find that not only is the job left behind but so, too, are those friendships that had grown within the business environment. Outside of the job you may discover that few common interests are shared. It can be like when your children have friends in school. During the days of their education the families of the kids tend to interact at sporting events and social get-togethers. But once the kids graduate they and their families tend to go in their own direction. Just as you learned to move on in that situation, so to may you need to be prepared to move on with regards to work based friendships.

The friendships we have established in work can continue to thrive outside of the job. My best friends were both people that I met originally on the job. We are still in regular contact although one lives in a different state. And as with any true friend all it takes is about five minutes before you are back on track like you just talked yesterday. It does take some effort but is well worth it.

But thinking back on the many others that I have worked with over the years it becomes apparent that we often move on once we say goodbye to the common bond of the job. While still a member of the working masses this was not much of an issue. When we left one job we could expect to meet new people at our next company and some percentage of those would become our new work friends. However, once there is no next job to look forward to the rules change.

In retirement your interests may be vastly different than while working. But as you try new things you can begin to meet similar minded people. You begin to build new relationships and make new friends. And these will be friends based on the person you are from this day forward regardless of any job.

Chapter 2 – Facing Retirement Fears

*If you look into your own heart, and you find
nothing wrong there, what is there to worry about?
What is there to fear? ~ Confucius*

The promise that sustains many through
challenging days is that vision of a future life to be
spent living a happy retirement doing what we
really want to be doing. Finally we will be
rewarded for all the scrimping and saving, the
sweat and toil of raising and nurturing a family,
and the putting aside of our individual desires for
the greater good of securing our future. Most will
agree that the journey here was not easy and yet if
we are able to successfully cross that finish line
into a victorious retirement it was all worthwhile.
And now that we have arrived there is nothing to
fear, right? The piper has been paid, the battle
fought and we have safely arrived into the arms of
our second act. But don't be too hasty in assuming
that everything is going to be just fine from this
point on.

When I look ahead to the promise of retirement I
have to admit that though optimistic, my outlook is
not all rosy. I have genuine concerns about just
how the next twenty or thirty years of my life will
play out. I know from experience that the
unexpected can wait just around the corner ready
to foul up an otherwise smooth retired life. If we
are not careful we may encounter a retirement life

filled with "I should have done that" or "I sure wasn't expecting this". Beyond the excitement and expectation, there are reasons we might view retirement with a bit of trepidation.

Running out of meaningful things to do

By nature I am someone who likes to keep busy. It is essential to my sanity that I remain engaged in a multitude of activities and distractions to keep my mind and body moving. I have learned to accept the fact that I just do not do well for long in a stationary position. Any attempts to sit in front of a TV to watch a three-hour-long football game will require at least two different books to choose between while the game progresses and an extended half time where I get outside to move around a bit. And so it is with a certain amount of concern that I contemplate how I will entertain myself during what I hope is an extended retirement life. Are there enough options, enough areas of possible interest out there to engage me for the next twenty years? Are there sufficient things that I feel passionate about, that inspire me and make each day worth getting out of bed? Or will I quickly run out of new and stimulating things to do? What I genuinely fear is starting on my way to living my retirement and suddenly finding myself bored, with few prospects for new and exciting avenues to pursue.

A reader of my blog shared her frustration with her situation and the challenges she faces trying to find meaning in the retired life she lives. *Lately I feel like I'm just going through the motions of life. I get up each day, walk the dogs, go to work, come home, walk the dogs and on it goes like a robot. I'm not sad, perhaps ambivalent. My kids are grown & have their own lives & I'm not a part of their lives. I feel I've had a good life, I'm still healthy but what's the point of sticking around & continuing this until my health fails.*

Many of us may like to think ourselves spontaneous and capable of filling our retirement dance card with an endless variety of enjoyable things to do. But have we really taken the time to think about exactly what that means? Have we honestly thought about what it is we will do for the next twenty or thirty years when there is no one telling us what to do? The scary reality is that some retirees to be spend more time planning for a week's vacation than for the many years of retired living they have in store.

Most of us can hope to experience a positive introduction into retirement, a happy honeymoon period during that first year or thereabouts after we jettison the working world and expectantly begin our new retired life. By the time we get there, most will typically have accumulated an impressive to-do list just begging to be attacked. Gardening projects that have been ignored can now be undertaken. Improvements and upgrades to house and hearth are ready and waiting. And how about that trip you have dreamed of for the past ten years? It is now time to pack your bags and get to it! Finally you have the chance to buy all of those wonderful books by favorite authors and experience the luxury of reading whichever you choose whenever you choose to do so. And when you are not busily pursuing your many interests you can take time to relax and enjoy living at a comfortable pace you set for yourself.

Then the honeymoon period begins to run its course. You might look back and rightly feel very satisfied in your accomplishments. You are caught up with your to-do list (congratulations!) including any additions post-retirement, you have enjoyed a handful of trips and adventures that had always been of interest, you are getting darn good at the whole relaxation side of it all and you find yourself peacefully settling into retired living. But as the weeks progress, don't be surprised to find yourself less excited about what your day has in store as those activities you have been engaged in might no longer be quite as interesting as they first were. Those relaxing afternoons can start to become tedious with little variety and nothing new to look forward to. Sure part of retirement living is slowing down but this is not likely what you had in mind. Tell tale signs that you may be heading down the wrong path include staying in bed a bit longer as there is nothing pressing to necessitate you getting up. You begin to find yourself watching the clock for the return of your spouse and should she be slightly late you become anxious. The television starts coming on earlier and earlier as you strive to fill the hours in the day. Tragically you can find yourself at a loss for things to do that matter and make you feel good about yourself. What to do?

Learning ways to address and mitigate this fear has been a focus on my blog *Retirement – Only the Beginning.* Basically what can we do to prepare to live a fulfilling, inspired retirement life beyond the focus on financial? What activities, practices, hobbies, studies, thoughts and passions can we discover that will fill our days with meaning? I sincerely believe that boredom can become a real problem for many in retirement unless we take time and make the effort to plan and prepare before we assume our roles as retirees. I invite you to visit the site at **http://LoveBeingRetired.com** to review a collection of posts covering what I have learned over the past years to better prepare to live that retirement life we all want. Why wait for boredom to overtake you when you can take the initiative and stay ahead of the curve?

For all of my fears of running out of meaningful things to occupy my day, there are those who find themselves quite busy in living their day-to-day retired life. In fact some to feel there is just not enough time in the day to get everything done. A blog reader laments *one of my biggest surprises was the way time speeds up. Not having to rise at a set time means that you rise later, spend more time over breakfast and the paper, move more slowly doing household tasks…and then the day is done!*

Another explains her challenge: *how quickly time goes by and how little we sometimes accomplish – there's always tomorrow. I felt guilty when I went shopping in the middle of the day. I taught first grade and still was afraid I'd run into a parent on "school time"! I've gotten over that!*

I am truly happy for these people and the busy, satisfying life they have discovered in retirement. At the pace they maintain there is little time for boredom. It is encouraging to know that living a busy day doing worthwhile activities is in fact doable. But until I experience this first hand, I will remain a bit fearful of running out of meaningful things to do when I retire.

Living with society's preconceptions about the elderly
Let's face it, growing old is not going to be easy. Perhaps the impact of challenges we must face can be slightly reduced by the fact that so many others are going through the same thing – we are not alone. 75 million baby boomers are beginning to join the ranks of the retired with 10,000 each day reaching age sixty five and continuing to do so for the next twenty years. Projections show the current 40 million senior citizens growing to 89 million by 2050. That is a lot of gray!

But although we are physically growing older, many are a long way from behaving elderly when it comes to attitude and zest for living. Members of the baby boomer generation have led lives different from their predecessors in various ways but one in particular. The careers of bygone years often required more demanding physical labor to perform the job at hand. As a result once the individual attained age sixty five he was pretty much spent. Retirement was not so much a luxury as a necessity, a time to rest tired bones after completing a physically tiring work career. Baby boomers are more likely to have careers that involve heavy mental rather than physical lifting. In their role as knowledge workers today's retirees to be can hope to coast more gently into retirement. Fewer have suffered through the burden of physical labor to the extent of earlier generations. Most importantly they can hope to maintain their mental sharpness for many years ahead baring disease or other outside influences. When it comes to productive and creative thinking, turning 65 is no longer the end of the line but in many cases just the beginning. Mike Wallace continued to broadcast on *60 Minutes* into his eighties. Frank Lloyd Wright didn't finish his design of the Guggenheim Museum until age 91. The world is beginning to discover that life is no longer over at 65.

Of course we should not downplay the physical effect a career packed with too much stress can have on a body. High blood pressure, poor sleep habits and the never ending pressure to climb the corporate ladder takes its toll. But in general I think it is reasonable to say that your typical knowledge worker is not physically done-in upon reaching retirement age. An increasing number will likely still have more to give. With energy left to burn and time on their hands these retirees may look into extending their careers or venturing down a new path to pursue an interest that previously lay dormant. Retirement can become a time to do things rather than a time to recover from things done. Today's retiree to be can hope to explore an exciting second act investigating a myriad of possible encore careers and other creative options.

The problem is that society seems to have other ideas, shall we say misperceptions about those aging in her ranks. A recent Oregon State study describes a general view that does not bode well for those of us soon to be counted amongst the elderly. "Our society devalues old age in many ways, and this is particularly true in the United States, where individualism, self-reliance, and independence are highly valued," says Oregon State University researcher Michelle Barnhart in a statement. "Almost every stereotype we associate with being elderly is something negative, from being 'crotchety' and unwilling to change to being forgetful."(2)

Would you take offense at being referred to as over-the-hill, out of touch, feeble, past your prime, stuck in the past, grumpy, blue hair, or perhaps that ever popular crotchety? I know that such categorizations rub me the wrong way. Sure I realize that at seventy I am probably not as svelte, smooth, sexy and sharp as I was at twenty but maybe in some ways I am better. It is so much about perception and being viewed as an antique doesn't cut it. This retiree to be hopes to have a lot to offer well beyond age 65. But before I complain too much about how I will be perceived, I need to be sensitive to those older than I. It is not impossible that during my younger years I may have referred to my elders in a less than flattering way – shame on me. As they say what goes around comes around and now I fear that as I age the world may view me as less than what I really am. Such thoughts make me a bit nervous as I consider my approaching retirement.

What if I am forced to retire before I am ready?

A very large number of boomers have already been pushed out of the workforce and are struggling to survive to age 65. The ones who are still working are hanging on for dear life as younger managers push for their jobs. There is also the sheer physical task of working past 60. Even with retirement, which is pretty much gone for most of us, it's hard to even move on some days.

If everything goes as I hope I will retire close to age 65, additionally feathering my nest egg over the remaining work years until I cross that bridge. If I can continue to save at my current rate (the kids have graduated and are on their own, the house is pretty much paid off, and credit card debt is not allowed), I can realistically hope to be relatively financially set to enjoy a reasonable retirement doing what I want to do. At least that is the plan.

However, as many are realizing the assumption of steady continuing employment is a big assumption in these challenging times. Companies are downsizing, technology is improving efficiency so fewer workers are required to deliver the same or better results, jobs are being sent offshore, and companies are merging left and right. Long term loyalty and dedication to a single company is becoming the stuff of fantasy. Many without work are finding themselves afloat in a job market over populated with highly qualified candidates willing to work for less than they are accustomed. And in the middle of all this turmoil we find the hard working middle age employee who has no choice but to ride the wave and hopefully not wipeout along the way.

Being suddenly unemployed at this stage of life is a legitimate fear. And once unemployed it just gets worse. If I do lose my job it is going to take longer to find a new one if I am fortunate enough to land anything. We read every day about retirement age people forced to take whatever job they can for minimum wage just trying to make ends meet. It is truly unnerving and for the aging population loss of a job is not restricted solely to economic vicissitudes or corporate policy but may also be the result of poor health issues. If we are no longer able to physically perform our job we will find ourselves out on the street.

There is a category that raises angst among baby boomers - the involuntary retired - those who are in their 60s and still want (and need) to work but can't find a job. I believe I've run smack into age discrimination which puts me in that category.

I try to be frugal when it comes to day to day living. I have ignored some of my personal wishes short term in order to prepare for that time when I will no longer be working. I have set goals that once achieved should provide for a reasonable retirement lifestyle. But if I unexpectedly find myself out of a job no longer able to make my planned contributions, my retirement plans will be at risk. Such thoughts can keep me awake at night.

Loneliness
I am married to a wonderful lady who makes me smile whenever I think of her. She is beautiful, smart, and inquisitive. She is an adventurous traveler who has infected me with that bug that can only be cured by visiting the world around us. She laughs at my jokes, accepts my faults, and is quick as a whip when we spar and playfully tease each other. I cannot wait for the time when we are

both retired and can together travel to our hearts content. I am blessed and I know it.

But there are many who may not have such a wonderful partner. There are those who look to retirement and see themselves alone. I remember watching a movie awhile ago where Bruce Willis played the central character, a retired guy, probably 60ish, living alone. One scene showed him eating a dinner of some canned food concoction piled high on his plate, not a sound to be heard except for his chewing, the room empty but for bare necessities, truly an uninspiring site. Not even the inane babble of a TV filtered through – there was no sound or sign of life outside of that room and that one lone character. At that moment I found myself asking if that was my life, if I was alone not just some of the time but most of the time, and if my tomorrow looked as bleak as today and yesterday, how would I cope. What would I do to survive loneliness?

It is pretty scary.

For some, being alone can be preferable to being stuck with someone who takes more effort than it is worth. Maintaining their own freedom to do what they want is how they choose to retire. They have a network of friends to interact with and keep busy with events of their choosing. They enjoy the freedom to explore their life passions as often as they want no matter what they may be. Rather than answer to the whims of another they make their decisions based upon their own counsel. At the end of the day they get to watch what they want on TV, eat what they want, and go to bed when they feel like it. It is not a bad life by any standards and those who live it can be quite happy.

But I need that love at my side to be happy. I cannot imagine a future that does not include my wife. I do not want to be alone and responsible for filling my second act with worthwhile activities and distractions. I am just not a good at being on my own.

Outliving my savings

Just yesterday I read a blog by a thirty-something woman bemoaning an underwater mortgage and the fear that she would never retire. I could only think that she was so wrong. "Get rid of that house and live on less than you can afford, save the difference and move on" would be the advice I would give her. She can retire if she lives within her means.

Do we have enough saved to comfortably provide for us during our retirement? Are the investments we have the right ones? What if there is another big 'adjustment' in the economy? Recessions come and go so it is not a matter of if but rather when the next rolls around. And should something catastrophic happen at an advanced age there will be far fewer options to catch up or recover.

I don't want to make the mistake of underestimating the number of years I will be retired. Can you imagine after a lifetime of planning and saving for retirement to miscalculate this mark to the extent that you outlive your retirement savings? What real options would there be at my senior age where I have been out of the workforce for so many years, am perhaps physically challenged and realistically not able to generate any additional income? Life expectancies are on the rise. By age 65 males in the United States have a 40 percent chance of reaching age 85 while females have a more than 50 percent chance.(3) Living a longer quality life is a blessing that earlier generations did not experience. But if you live longer you will need to plan accordingly or risk underestimating your retirement needs.

Challenges of declining health
Virgil said, *"The greatest wealth is health."* Although the twenty something youth may scoff at this statement you can bet that to the sixty something gentleman nothing rings truer. When we are young we can take good health for granted. As we age we are forced to accept that things are not as they once were despite how we may feel on the inside. The other day I was walking my neighborhood when I spotted a dime on the ground. I stopped for a moment to stare intently but made no move to pick up the coin. It dawned on me that I was analyzing the effort required to bend down for the ten cents and had

come to the conclusion that it was not worth it. At that moment I knew I was no longer a kid but was in fact entering into the ranks of the oldsters. A younger me would not have hesitated to swoop down and scoop up that dime, actually any coin of any denomination. Not so any longer. I shook my head knowingly, a bit sadly, and walked on. But I made the internal commitment that should I spy a quarter on the ground, I would pick it up. Of course who can say if twenty five cents will be worth the effort ten years down the line?

The reality is that we will slow down as we age. Physically and mentally things begin to wear out. Bit by bit, step by step, inch by inch life can become slightly more challenging than in days gone by. Each of us individually will need to come to grips with this situation. Perhaps we may find some solace in the fact that no one escapes the effects of time. Friends and family are all in for the same ride. I get it and am doing my best to come to terms with it.

What I fear is getting to a point where physical limitations interfere with the most basic pleasures and life experiences. I do not want to find myself too tired to go on walks with my wife through the neighborhood. I don't want to have to give up my workouts because my joints are too sore or muscles too weak. I cannot imagine life with vision so poor that I am unable to read the books I love. I fear the day when the hassles of airplane travel become too great so that we choose to stay at home. I am not looking forward to the time when the effort to put up a Christmas tree outweighs the promise of its wonderful pine smell and sparkling lights.

Yes I can logically accept that getting older will take a toll. What scares me is just what that toll may ultimately be.

Dependence on others

One of the reasons baby boomers are waiting longer for retirement is that we do not want to be a burden on our family members when it comes to a time we cannot fend for ourselves. We hopefully will be able to pay for assisted care living or nursing homes through our estates. The last thing we want is to be a burden on our children.

Once I completed my college education, I found an affordable little studio in a not so desirable neighborhood and began my life as an independent self-sufficient member of society. My folks had taken care of me to this point paying for my schooling and living expenses and I remain forever in their debt (fortunately interest free). They did their part and it was my turn to take responsibility for my future. It was exciting, it was a bit scary, but it was a good thing for all concerned.

Independence is a beautiful thing. With it we are afforded the ability to navigate our way through life following a path that we choose. Good decisions along with bad are part of the journey but they are our decisions, we make them, and we live with the consequences. We still depend on others for various things but generally in a peripheral sort of way. At our core, what we are and who we are is reflected in our own independent action and effort. The greatest thing about independence is the feeling that we are in control, the future is up to us, and if it needs to get done we can do it.

After so many years of taking care of myself and following my own rules the thought of giving it all up scares me. Should the time come when I am no longer able to safely take care of myself, I could be forced to hand over the keys of my life to others. They will decide what is best for me, where I should live, what I should eat, how I should live this life of mine. I would hope to still offer input but even that may prove not to be the case. Although doing what they believe is in my best interest, how can anyone really know exactly what I want? Only I can see within myself and make those most appropriate choices. But at some point they may no longer be mine to make.

While raising my children I was always the rock, the strong dad able to leap tall buildings in a single bound. If there was a problem, run to dad – he will know what to do. Moving into a new place? Better get dad to help with the heavy stuff. Trying to handle life challenges for the first time and finding it tough? You can bet dad will listen and know just the right thing to say. There was a time when all roads led to dad and there was not a happier person on this earth than that dad. The unfortunate reality of this aging thing is there may come a time when that great and powerful dad will need to lean on his children. I am okay with a little leaning. What scares me is if the time should come when my leaning becomes a burden on my kids. I appreciate a helpful hand as much as anyone but the idea of someone other than me running my life is not something I really like to dwell upon.

Weathering the next recession

During the recessions of recent years I was employed fulltime. Just like everyone else, my investments took a hit, the value of our home dropped, and the typical feeling in my stomach is best described as what you experience when you take that vertical plunge from the top of the rollercoaster and plunge downward at breakneck speed. And yet the fact that I was still working and still able to put money into our future was a refuge and sanity saver.

Now as a retiree the rules have changed. We all know it is just a matter of time before the next recession or depression or other financial 'event' occurs, the consequences and magnitude of which are yet to be determined. Removed from the working world I will be that much more impacted by such an occurrence. Without the ability to replace losses with additional earnings I will be forced to sit on the sidelines and pray for a happy ending. I read recently that the baby boomers were the generation most damaged by our recent recession. Losses in retirement investments and home values happened at a terrible time as many were just starting to move into retirement. And at the same time many are supporting both children as well as parents, a double whammy. Many retirement plans have to be put on hold as people work more years to replace losses. But if you are already retired and job opportunities are slim you may not have this option.

So we weathered this recession and the one before. But if I am retired when the next one happens I am afraid of the consequences and my ability to counter them.

As you can see my fears regarding retirement are not simply paranoia. And yet I do not want to obsessively focus on the negatives as there is so much positive as well. I truly look forward to my retirement despite the challenges and pitfalls that may wait. A reader of my blog helped put it in perspective as she explained her retirement experience:

You talk about retiring as if it was something to be apprehensive about – why? I am fast approaching 68 and have been retired since I was sixty. Apart from putting my finances in order for my retirement, I have never really given this phase of my life much thought.

I have children and grandchildren. I have worked all my life and have also had a great deal of interests outside these spheres. For me retirement was just another phase in life and one in which I could do all the things I enjoyed whenever I wanted to. I have always loved writing and now I have made this into a second career, but on my terms. I am my own boss and I take time off without asking anyone else.

If you approach retirement with apprehension you will never enjoy it. Even if the finances are not all that they should be, remember that you went to school and learned to write. Use this ability to top up your finances occasionally and find yourself in the centre of life and really living

There is hope for us all!

Chapter 3 – Building your Personal Custom Retirement

Life isn't about finding yourself. Life is about creating yourself. ~ George Bernard Shaw

Retirement is defined quite simply and succinctly in Wikipedia as *the point where a person stops employment completely.* To those about to begin their personal journey into retired living that abbreviated account might seem an understatement of sorts. As 75 million baby boomers begin to enter that time in their lives when retirement becomes a consideration if not a priority, retirees to be may quickly discover there is a lot more to consider beyond simply the absence of work. Talk about a life changing event – no more nine-to-five, no more Monday morning dread, no more corporate politics, away with those boring meetings, done with pressure filled project deadlines, and finally time for ourselves to do what we want to do. Rather than centering our efforts on moving up in the ranks we can begin to focus on moving out into the world and on to brand new experiences. Retirement can change the way we live every day and redefine those activities we have become accustomed to doing during that day. There is a bit more to retirement than merely the absence of employment.

Well before reaching the threshold of retirement the wise retiree to be will begin to navigate the endless jungle of details that promises to make up his retired life. Assuming we retire at 65 the duration of our typical retirement will be in the twenty to thirty year range. That is a lot of days, a lot of weeks, and a lot of months during which we are solely responsible for identifying and pursuing interests to make our days worth living. Gone are those busy working days filled with packed calendars. Our weekends will extend beyond Saturday and Sunday to include the entire seven day week. Imagine the possibilities now that we can pursue our passions and plans seven days a week! Get ready for time on our hands – lots of it.

I retired from years working in social services and now am following my own bliss. I have a small antique business that I started the month after my retirement. I love old things and the search for them. For the first time in my life I am able to wake up when I want, and the way I spend my day is up to me. I am free to be me.

As we look toward our future, it can help to start to prepare for what is going to happen rather than just wait and see. There might be actions we can take ahead of time to provide for an even more enjoyable retired life. Try to visualize your perfect retirement. Based upon the person you are, your interests and your passions, how might your perfect retirement look? Try to picture what is really right for you. It is never too early to begin planning for your own fulfilling retirement. Once you more clearly understand where you are today and where you want to ultimately end up, you can start putting together the pieces to build a retirement custom made for you.

What does retirement mean to me?

So you have decided it is time to call it quits at the old job and take a step into a new life of retirement, a new chapter, a new beginning. Some soon to be retirees find themselves almost giddy with excitement and expectation as they look toward the wonderful new life they will soon begin. Others are just ready for a break from the same old grind. Still others may find themselves a bit unsure and perhaps nervous about exactly what lies ahead. With the pending event drawing ever nearer, ideally you are beginning to ask the questions that will give you a deeper understanding of your personal views and expectations.

How do you feel about retirement?

Are you ready or reluctant?

How do you envision yourself in the next five years? What about ten? What about 20?

Are you optimistic or pessimistic about your new life ahead?

Are you maybe a bit scared? If so what is it that concerns you? What are your biggest fears?

What most excites you about the promise of retirement?

Are you looking forward to exploring new interests and trying different things?

Are you creative and energetic enough to occupy yourself with meaningful events each day?

Are you looking forward to spending 24/7 with your spouse?

Will you be able to find meaning in a life outside of work?

What single thing do you believe is most important to achieving happiness in retirement?

An understanding today of what you expect in retirement can allow you to make adjustments while you still have time.

Take a look at your emotional reasons for working (doing something worthwhile, being respected by others, etc.). Those don't just drive your work, they drive your life. You need to find non-work interests that give you the same sort of emotional benefits.

While I was searching for just the right cover for this book, I asked myself what single picture would best represent the concept of retirement. Is it even possible for a single moment in time to summarize all that is part and parcel of retired life? What I did not want to do was go with the old tried and true snapshots typically associated with retired life. I did not want to use a sunset since I believe that retirement is the beginning of something new rather than the end. I was not interested in using one of the many pictures of an old couple sitting on a bench looking out at a beautiful view of ocean, lake, or mountains. Yes this can be a wonderful component of the retirement we will live but it downplays all of the activity and adventure and life there is to live in addition to watching the world go by. And I sure wasn't going to use a picture of someone swinging a club on the golf course, a far to frequent depiction of what awaits the recent retiree.

I settled on the picture you see of an empty hammock swinging in the breeze. First of all the vacant spot invites someone to climb on in and enjoy a peaceful, relaxing moment and who better qualified than a happily retired person in search of a little downtime. Secondly, the fact that the location is a tropical spot on some unknown shore reflects the myriad of options we will have to travel and explore new and exotic locales once we retire. The hammock may await us but not before the adventure of getting there has been lived. Finally, I have always had a thing for the ocean and the peace it brings to my soul. I can definitely picture myself reclining in the hammock, gently swaying in the warm tropical breezes with the steady sound of waves breaking in the distance. And when I am ready, one quick hop out of my hammock and a new unexplored world awaits me.

At what age will I retire?

Ask yourself these three questions:

Do I have enough?
Have I had enough?
Do I have enough to do?

For some the decision of when to retire will be made for them. Health issues may come into play and if you are no longer able to perform your job effectively, you must depart. Or changes in your role or position occur and you lose your job. Sometimes the company where you have worked for years comes to the end of the line and shuts its doors. Finding yourself middle aged and out of a job can present a serious challenge to finding new employment.

For retirees who are able to choose the time of their retirement there are numerous variables to consider. You will want to review and carefully determine when to begin receiving your social security payments. The earliest you can begin collecting benefits is age 62 however if you start then, you will receive only 75 percent of what you would qualify for at full retirement age. For those born between 1943 and 1954 full retirement age is 66. If you wait until age 70 you will be entitled to the maximum monthly payment. Social Security checks will grow by 8 percent for each year you delay claiming beyond your full retirement age, up until age 70. Waiting beyond age 70 does not increase your payment. Note that according to the Social Security Administration site, if you live the average life expectancy for someone your age you will receive about the same amount in lifetime benefits whether you choose to begin receiving benefits at 62 or 70 or anywhere in between.(4)

A reader of my blog shared a helpful perspective: *Every year I work past 65 (now almost 69) and collect benefits is a double dipping year. Earn money, save money, and not withdraw from modest retirement nest egg has me wanting to stay in the work force. I only plan to modestly reduce time in a year or two. And I don't feel guilty about spending on vacations or other vanity items (camera lens, iPhone and weekly meals out).*

Along with your social security calculations you will want to determine when you can actually afford to retire. When will your savings and investments and the income they generate be sufficient to cover your expenses and support your desired retirement lifestyle so you will not have to work for money again? Important variables to consider include sufficient healthcare coverage as insurance and medical rates continue to increase, sufficient cushion should the economy take a tailspin which based upon its historical cyclical nature is just a matter of time, enough to allow you to live a meaningful and fulfilling retirement with travel and excitement and fun, and consideration for your personal tolerance of risk when it comes to your portfolio. Take your time and be thorough with your calculations as you do not want to overlook any significant details. Unless you are comfortable with the overwhelming complexity of retirement planning from a financial perspective, it can make good sense to enlist the help of a professional. Look for someone who takes the time to intimately understand you and your situation, asking the right questions and analyzing all the options before offering any specific recommendations. Such an advisor will be available for regular updates and to address changes in your circumstances over time. Your biggest risk is not what your investments will do in the next quarter but rather what they will do over the next 10 or 20 or more years.

Another consideration when planning your retirement date is your personal as well as family health history. A history of health issues can impact the length of time you will be able to continue working. If there is an increased likelihood you might experience health issues sooner rather than later, you will want to factor that into your estimated time for retirement. I believe it is wise no matter what the situation to enjoy some of your dreams and adventures along the way rather than save everything for after you retire. No one knows what life has in store for us. It would be tragic to slave and save all your life only to find yourself unable to enjoy your retirement years due to some ailment or condition beyond your control.

Try to coordinate the time of your retirement with your spouse's plans. Do you want to retire at the same time? Will one of you retire before the other to test the waters and prepare the way? This may make sense where the difference in ages is significant. If one of you continues working you can take advantage of medical coverage as well as continue contributing to retirement plans to the extent you can afford to do so. Discuss the options and see if you can agree upon what is best for your particular situation.

Do I want work to be a part of my retirement?

I think that on-again-off-again retirement may be the wave of the future. Honestly, I do not think that any human being should "quit working". The need to be productive is a part of life.

For some, financial considerations are such that they will be forced to continue working in some capacity. It has been a rough bunch of years recently and many have seen their nest egg depleted with savings reduced, investments savaged and property values shrunk. Retirement age can be a taunting concept when the likelihood of retiring is unrealistic now or in the foreseeable future.

But for the fortunate, working is a choice they are able to make. If you do not have to work why would you choose to work? There are numerous benefits realized working with others. There is a camaraderie that develops between co-workers who are working toward common goals. We have someone to talk to, to share our lives and find support. For many retirees the biggest thing they miss and one of the top reasons they seek to return to work is to experience that interaction with others.

Having a job also means that each day you have somewhere to go and something to do. Some retirees may feel like a ship without a rudder when it comes to finding worthwhile activities to engage in. Left to their own resources they may quickly run out of options and risk the curse of boredom. There is a certain security to be found in the knowledge that during those hours on the job you will be busily engaged.

And as an experienced employee you have the opportunity to share your knowledge and mentor those less experienced than you. As the company grows and new faces pour in, your expertise along with firsthand knowledge of the history and culture of the company make you a valuable resource. And what fun to work with young, excited and energetic co-workers and see them mature and become successful, even if they end up becoming your boss!

Mature workers may have skills and abilities younger workers do not yet have, provide mentoring for the next generation and as long as they stay healthy and active, it may be a plus for younger workers. With a lifespan of 85-95, we don't want to put talented and creative people on the shelf for 20 years. And what a bore that would be.

If you decide that there is a place for work in your retirement, another consideration is whether you want to remain in your chosen career or experiment with something new. This transitional time could be the perfect opportunity to pursue a new and exciting path.

And how about this out of the box idea: if you like the positive aspects of work but do not want to commit the rest of your life, you may consider working in an on-again-off-again combination. For example, you might find yourself working for a nice company, enjoying the interaction with co-workers and taking home a little additional cash. After a year or two or whatever period fits your situation, you decide you have had enough and want to exit for awhile. You take some time to travel and pursue other interests whether a few months or a few years, again depending on your plans. Then, once you are recharged and ready to re-engage you look for the next work opportunity and repeat the cycle. Taking time away from the job gives you the chance to refresh yourself and get back on track, something that benefits both you and your next employer. Engaging in a variety different jobs allow you to experiment a bit with your different interests. And best of all during that time off you are able to retire short term for as long as you choose and enjoy your freedom. What a perfect combination of working and not working! The danger is that when you are ready to get back into the job market there may not be opportunities that fit your skills or requirements. But if you can make it work, how sweet would it be?

What activities and pursuits do I most enjoy?
Since as a soon-to-be-retiree you are about to have the freedom to do whatever you want to do, what are your favorite things? Now that your pool of possibilities is limitless, what will you choose? And don't be overly conservative. Retirement can be the perfect chance to step outside of your comfort zone and consider the many possibilities.

Upon first examination most of us can pretty easily come up with a list of short term interests. Some examples might include gardening, home improvements, daily walks, reading, etc. These are the typical activities that we may have been unable to sufficiently address during our pre-retirement life. And although these activities represent an important component of your daily retired life, they are only one piece.

What can also be helpful is to identify pursuits that are more meaningful, that may give you a feeling of fulfillment upon completion, things that when you look back at the end of the day make you feel you have accomplished something. Finding a way to share time between short term activities and more meaningful undertakings can help provide a more balanced retired day.

While you are at it think about how you can incorporate relaxation into your productive activities. For many retirees the promise of a peaceful existence away from the stress of work is just what retirement is all about. Well earned rewards can include sleeping in as long as we want, enjoying that second cup of coffee with no pressure to get on with your day, working out during the day when the mood hits you, reading a book when you feel like reading a book, and generally progressing at a pace that best suits you for that particular moment.

Downtime is an important variable in our retirement life. We finally have time to slow down and step back from the craziness that has been life to this point. Again it is a matter of balance. If our entire focus is on doing as little as possible there is a chance that eventually we may become bored. How many days on end can we watch life rather than engage in living it? How we balance our day between relaxation and activity is up to our personal taste.

Do I want to relocate?
Some may find retirement the perfect catalyst to spur a move to new digs. Along with the changes brought on by living a new retired life, this can be a chance to consider moving to that idyllic location you have contemplated over the years. You no longer must live near your work. The family is in general grown and on about their own lives. Ideally your mortgage is paid off or close to that point. You have the freedom to make the choice of

staying where you are or relocating if you so desire.

Why would you want to relocate in retirement? As with any other part of your retirement planning it depends on what is important to you. Your personal interests and motivations, life situation, need for change and willingness to take a chance all influence your decision. One of my blog readers offered a helpful suggestion to help prioritize your requirements: *I'd suggest that the retiree make three lists – "Must haves," "Nice to haves," and "Definitely don't wants." The "Must haves" are those characteristics of an ideal retirement place which are most important, those which the retiree is unwilling to compromise. The "Nice to haves," are the factors which the retiree would prefer to have, but about which he or she would make some compromise. The "Definitely don't wants," are characteristics of a community which, for the individual retiree, are deal breakers. That is, they absolutely wouldn't consider moving to a community which has those specific characteristics.*

If you are contemplating relocation, here are some factors that might influence your disposition toward making a move:

Improve your financial situation
You may feel that the cost of living where you currently reside is beyond what you will be comfortable with in retirement. Income taxes can

differ by location. Pensions may be taxed differently or not at all as is the case for Massachusetts and Alabama. Property taxes vary by state and can improve your overall financial picture if you choose carefully. If you are able to effectively swap your existing home for your new without paying more, so much the better. And for the truly adventurous a move to a foreign country can offer a lower cost of living while opening up a whole new world to explore.

Experience that small town environment
If you have lived and worked in a big city you have endured the good as well as the bad. For some the heavy toll taken by years of traffic, painfully slow commutes, lengthy lines for everything, and people who seem distant or even afraid can outweigh the cultural diversity and social events offered by metropolitan areas. Instead they find they prefer a small town where they support local business and interact with people who know your name or at least make eye contact as you pass on the street.

Get closer to Mother Nature
Have you always dreamed of living closer to nature? Do you entertain thoughts of awaking to the babble of a nearby river or the calming pound of waves on the beach? Do you prefer the sound of birds singing to the noise of horns honking? Is green your choice over stainless steel? If so this can be your chance to get closer to what you truly enjoy.

Try something new

If you have lived a significant portion of your life in the same surroundings, maybe you are ready for a change. This can be the perfect opportunity to step outside your comfort zone and explore. Since a permanent move is a big commitment you may opt to rent for awhile in the area you are considering. Get the real scoop from behind the scenes as you interact with the locals, wander the neighborhoods and downtown establishments, and explore neighborhood attractions and amenities. Then if you decide this is the right place you and your partner can take the next steps.

We recently returned from our annual trip to Cabo del Sol in Baja Mexico. Each year we spend a week in a beautiful area that is about five miles north of the busy party central Cabo San Lucas. That distance is perfect for us as our party hardy days are a thing of the past and we prefer the peaceful sound of waves to the pounding music of downtown. Cabo offers just the right combination for my wife and me as the ocean and waves are what make me most content while the warm sun keeps her in a perpetually happy mood. We have found the locals incredibly friendly and the slower pace a refreshing change from the working life we are accustomed to. The cost of living is more affordable and housing options will not bankrupt us. The thought of retiring to this location for at least a portion of the year is very tempting. And with the years of high school Spanish still salvageable in this brain of mine (plus my wife can speak the language), who knows?

Prepare for old age
If you have health issues or concerns, relocating to a community that is senior-friendly may be a consideration. Retirement communities these days are filled with activities, special events, facilities and staff that are knowledgeable in all things senior. Sometimes it makes sense to make the move to these communities earlier rather than later. There is enough to keep you busy and engaged while you get used to the surroundings and become familiar with the natives.

On the flip side, what will you sacrifice if you decide to move elsewhere? Unfortunately you will leave behind the relationships you have established with your neighbors. Despite the best intentions it can be challenging although not impossible to maintain those friendships long distance. But when you take a look around the old neighborhood, it is often the case that many of those long term neighbors are also moving to new locales. If your family is nearby, your relocation may distance you from them just when you finally have time to spend together. Those people and resources that make up your current support network cannot easily be transferred. You will need to re-establish these ties in your new home. You will also have to build new relationships with doctors and hospitals.

When you relocate you will have to say goodbye to the house where over the years you have lovingly created the surroundings just to your liking. That perfect garden, those carefully matched drapes and furniture, the kitchen you know so well – all will be left behind. It is not easy to abandon after so many years what has been known as home. Of course you can replicate your favorite features to some extent in your new house if you choose. And don't overlook the fact that this could be the perfect opportunity to create in your house that living environment you have dreamed of, one that is at the same time better suited for the changes you will experience as you age.

You will leave behind the old restaurants and stores, coffee shops and local parks that you have grown to love. Say goodbye to those comfortable familiar places where your presence elicits a smile or better yet a first name welcome. Adios to those places that made your favorite dishes just the way you liked them. You will have to rediscover these in your new neighborhood.

For some there is an additional consideration which is the option to purchase a second home. What can be attractive about this option is your ability to choose where you want to live for any given portion of the year. You can live where the weather is most to your liking and should the situation change, head back to your alternate digs. Or if you need a change in surroundings you can head out to your home behind door number two and experience the variety in their local neighborhoods and attractions. My wife and I throw around the idea of a second place in either Switzerland where we would spend awesome summers or Arizona where we are almost guaranteed warmer winters. We like the idea of maintaining our current home in the Bay Area which is big enough for our family needs and includes a nice backyard with recently upgraded interior. The central location gives us easy access to San Francisco as well as airports to the north and south of us. This we consider our home base from which we hope to head off on new adventures abroad.

What has given us reason to take pause when considering a second home is most significantly the purchase cost followed closely by the ongoing maintenance requirements of a home where we would live only part time. We do not necessarily like the idea of renting the place when we are not there so can count on any help with the mortgage. And where ever the location, maintenance and upkeep and repairs will be on going. How frustrating it would be to receive a phone call that heavy snows had collapsed the roof of your second home and you living a few thousand miles away need to fix it as soon as possible. At least for now we will stick with the idea of renting a place somewhere interesting, paying our fees to the owner and maintaining the freedom to return if it was a positive experience or move on to the next interesting locale.

I'd suggest that the person newly retired not be in a hurry to move. The decision to stay put for a year or so gives the retiree the opportunity to test out retirement without introducing other variables. It seems to me a good idea to make just one major change at a time. The retiree can first see how it feels to be retired. At the end of the year (more or less), the retiree will then be able to make a more informed decision regarding relocation.

As with many retirement decisions there are pluses and minuses when considering whether to stay in place or relocate. The good news is that as a retiree to be, you have some time as well as freedom to consider the choices that will best fit your plans.

What am I most passionate about?

Since retirement will be a time in your life when you have the ability to do what you want to do, what is it that you want to do more than anything else? Some call it finding meaning or purpose in what you do, a reason for being. I like to call it passion. The dictionary defines passion as *an intense or vehement emotion, occupying the mind in great part for a considerable period, and commanding the most serious action of the intelligence.* It is our passion that drives us, inspires us, empowers us and can ultimately give our lives meaning beyond merely existing. If I can pursue my passions without distraction I am more likely to find myself anxious to get out of bed each morning and get to it. If what I am doing each day is what I love to do could it get any better? A retirement focused on pursuing our individual passions has the potential to be very fulfilling.

Do you know what you are passionate about? In my earlier book *Are You Just Existing and Calling it a Life?* I propose a series of questions to help better define what it is you might be most passionate about including the following:

What do you value?

What excites you?

What subjects fascinate you?

What do you find most meaningful in your life?

What is important to you?

Who is your hero? Why?

When you were a child what was your greatest dream? What did you want to become?

What drives you?

What is it that when you explain to others gets them just as excited as you?

Who are the most important people in your life?

What of your skills do you most enjoy using?

What would your perfect job look like?

Once you have figured out what are your passions there is one more very important question – are you pursuing those passions? Now that you are retired, what is stopping you from living that life you want? If you can identify what you are most passionate about and if you can build into your retirement life the pursuit of those passions you can hope to look forward to quality times and meaningful moments along your journey.

Chapter 4 - Accepting Aging

To be seventy years young is sometimes far more cheerful and hopeful than to be forty years old.
~ Oliver Wendell Holmes

Say it isn't so. Out walking the other morning, I glanced down at my short-pant-clad legs and saw something new. The last time I looked at my legs I could have sworn I saw nicely toned, could-be-a-little-more-tanned thighs supporting my body. Today I swear I saw the legs of an older man. Nothing drastic but you know how the skin seems to have been over stretched just a bit and is not clinging as tightly to the muscles beneath? Then it dawned on me that I might no longer be among the ranks of the young and beautiful people but instead was knocking tentatively on the door of old age.

How was it possible for aging to catch up with me? I have been an exercise fanatic since college and even today have a regular routine. I ride the stationary bike three or four times a week for 40 minutes with my heart rate around 130-140, I lift weights twice a week, I do a Yoga and Pilates routine twice a week, and on Saturday and Sunday, my wife and I take long walks in the nearby hills or along the beach. We eat well avoiding fat and too much salt, go organic whenever we can, and pay attention to our portion size. You would think a healthy routine for sure but

I guess when it comes to aging you can run but you cannot hide.

I consider myself an optimist but at the same time a realist. I accept the facts for what they are and do my best to go with the flow. This aging thing is just another part of my life that I need to learn to accept and come to grips with.

Henri Amiel said, *"To know how to grow old is the master-work of wisdom and one of the most difficult chapters in the great art of living."* Unless we live in a bubble we have all witnessed the progression of fellow inhabitants of planet Earth as they move from youth into middle age to older and ultimately on to just plain old. Whether parents or grandparents or neighbors or just that old person we walk past on the park bench, older citizens are everywhere. An impressive number of 10,000 baby boomers will reach age 65 every day and continue to do so for the next twenty years assuring that if anything there will only be more oldsters on hand.

I feel like a 60 year old semi-educated idiot who can't seem to take advantage of the time he has and the blessing of not having huge financial problems. Still, this new life has become like a condition I can't seem to accept, understand or shake.

How do you come to terms with aging when on the inside you still feel like that younger version of you? Who among us wants to be that white haired senior citizen commonly depicted on TV plodding stiffly through life? Everyone would prefer to be that young, wrinkle-free, fresh face, ever-so-perky model that graces the screen and media. Young is where it is at or at least so Madison Avenue endlessly preaches. Everywhere we look we are bombarded with products that promise to make us look and feel younger, erase unsightly wrinkles, renew and improve our sex drive, make us smarter and taller, etc. If even a small percentage of the get-young advertisements actually did what they claim, we would be hard pressed to spot a senior citizen anywhere in the population at large! I would venture that most of us will find ourselves caught up to some degree in all the hype around staying young. And I don't think it is necessarily a problem if we experiment with a little cream or try a magical supplement or give the latest how-to-stay-young-and-desirable program a shot. Heck what can it hurt?

What can be a problem is when we go too far and become obsessed with staying forever young. It is sad when misguided people cling desperately to youth with extravagant and expensive plastic surgeries that change their look so much that friends hardly recognize them. It is disheartening to see an older woman buried in too much makeup while wearing a skirt too short for her age in efforts to look like her daughter. It is comical to see the old guy shrunken down in the seat of his sexy sports car struggle to exit without aid of a helping hand or nearby crane.

There is a time and a place for being young just as there is a time and a place for aging. Denial and delusions will only go so far. And if we took a moment to seriously look we would realize that our attempts to maintain eternal youth are rather transparent to those around us. Despite our efforts the real us tends to shine through.

What we can all use is a way to come to grips with the reality that we are getting older. There are things we can do and attitudes we can assume that might help make this aging thing less intimidating. Perhaps we can learn to accept the challenges along with the promises that will be a part of our lives as senior citizens.

Years ago a friend shared with me a tip she'd learned at a conference on aging, one that I truly enjoy practicing. "Every day try to do one thing you have never done before." It's really not that difficult. It turns out that sources of pleasure around us are endless.

Limitations are the reality

Do you sometimes find yourself asking "when did I get too old to do that?" You swear to yourself that it was just days ago when you were last able to complete the same task but maybe it was in actuality a bit longer than that. We have a rule in our house called the "double-time factor". Basically if it seems like two years ago the real timeframe was more likely double that or four years ago. I find as I get older it helps to have little formulas and tricks to keep things straight.

Getting older can make everything a bit more challenging whether reading road signs or walking stairs or bending down to pick up a dropped book. It is the nature of things and there is no escape, no asking for mercy. Denial is not an option. My mom went for years ignoring the hints of family and friends that perhaps her hearing may not be as sharp as it once was. She finally came to the realization that she needed help when she could not make out what her bridge partner was bidding. After a quick visit to the doctor and the installation of a slick almost invisible hearing aid she is back on top of her game much to the delight of her partner and family. The sooner we begin to accept the limitations that typically come with old age the better we can hope to face the coming day.

As our environment starts to give us a hard time we do not need to stand idly by. We can make a difference with something as minor as putting stronger bulbs in lamps to improve visibility around the home. Or perhaps a more significant undertaking like replacing front steps with a ramp, adding railings to the bathtub or swapping door knobs for handles that are easier to manage. Ignoring potential dangers can have dire consequences so it helps to be proactive and fix them first. Doing what we can to improve the situation might also give a feeling of empowerment to overcome that helplessness we may be becoming all too familiar with.

Not all things will be easy along our retired life's path but we can try to do our part to improve the situation. Realizing we may not be able to do everything on our own, we can learn to reach out to others for help. Limitations may be a reality but they need not be treated as impassable roadblocks to living a fulfilling retirement.

Sometimes you need to laugh at yourself
Try not to take yourself too seriously. People prefer a sincere smiling face to a frown every time. When you can laugh at yourself you expose the real you with all your vulnerabilities as well as strengths. You want to be comfortable enough with yourself and who you are to just let go. Not always serious, not always with-it, not always perfect, but a real, living, breathing human being.

If you take yourself too seriously the many challenges to be dealt with in retirement might become overwhelming. Sometimes you need to laugh when you really feel like crying about the injustice of it all.

The other side of the coin is making others laugh. It does not matter what the context as long as it is not at someone else's expense. Laughing is truly contagious. It starts with a little smile and broadens as it engages more of the face, ultimately resulting in a carefree, happy, stress-releasing tee-hee or guffaw or deep belly laugh. I do not believe it is physically possible to not feel good yourself when you make someone else laugh – it is simply against the laws of nature! Take it from someone who has spent most of his life endeavoring to make those around him smile and laugh. I don't know exactly what it is but it sure feels good.

Don't be that grumpy old man

Want to know what you can do to become known as a grumpy old person? One way is to honk your horn relentlessly on the road. When someone ahead of you is driving too slowly, honk your horn. If another driver makes an unexpected turn, hit the horn again. And woe the dallying driver who does not shoot through the intersection immediately upon a green light—he will hear the wrath of your honk. When we find ourselves using the horn as our main means of communication on the road, it may be time to take a closer look in the mirror.

It's funny. Now that I'm retired I'm the one everyone is always honking at because I'm never in a hurry. But everyone else sure is!

You may be perceived as a grumpy old man if you tend to overly focus on the bad rather than the good. If a grandchild fills your weekend with many joyous moments, but all you remember is that she spilled grape juice on the rug, you are missing the point. If a sunny week should end with one overcast day and that is what you focus on, you need a reset. Dwight D. Eisenhower said, *"Pessimism never won any battle."* Don't let an outlook of doom and gloom undermine what can be an excellent retirement.

Praise rather than condemn

The other day an acquaintance proudly brought to my attention the new dress she was wearing, fishing innocently for a compliment. I thought it was hideous. I could have called it like I saw it, but instead I mentioned how flattering her hair was, deflecting an arrow. The results were quickly apparent on her happy face.

Can you remember a time when you paid a compliment to a child and their resulting joy? It does not have to be something big just something. How easy is it to utter a few words of encouragement and praise yet how far reaching can be the impact. As a senior with the experience of years we would hope that what we say would be valued by others (not always the case but it should be). If we focus on the positives rather than the negatives and express our admiration for a deed well done we might raise the spirits of those around us who respect our wisdom.

Only old on the outside

I think there is an important step when it comes to how we deal with aging. This step is – I'm not going down easy. I accept the inevitable but I plan to fight for all its worth with whatever I have. No giving up or accepting that today needs to be any worse than yesterday. Maybe I'm just a fool but I won't waste time feeling sorry for myself.

Looking at a child playing in the park we form a clear image in our mind of the energetic, fun-loving, perpetually moving creature that lives within the little body. Cast a similar glance toward a senior citizen and what do you see? I would venture that based on external appearance you expect the older person to be a bit slow, set in their ways, occasionally grumpy, and far from energetic. As a retiree to be, we may soon find ourselves classified in that same group as others are challenged to see beyond the wrinkles to the person within.

Senior citizens face many challenges ranging from threats of falling to worsening eyesight, from poorer hearing to bad balance – the list goes on. But inside most still burns the fire to live and love, to learn and experience life, and to share happiness and survive sadness. We should let that inner us out and share the life and passion that still flows within. Samuel Ullman said, *"Nobody grows old merely by living a number of years. We grow old by deserting our ideals. Years may wrinkle the skin, but to give up enthusiasm wrinkles the soul."* We should try to uncork the bottle wherein sleeps the genie of our youthful self. It is unwise to restrain what is fighting to be set free. Let's make some noise, stir things up a bit, be a little outrageous, and show this world that we are alive and kicking.

Have you gone to see any of the bands from the seventies and eighties that have begun to tour again? My wife and I recently attended a concert to hear a group I first saw when I was in high school. Most of the singers were in their late sixties and early seventies and they looked every bit their age. Although voices were not quite so sharp and the ranges a bit reduced, the enjoyment and excitement they felt was apparent. They went at it with a gusto and passion that quickly spread to the crowd and made for a fun evening for all. They may look old on the outside but they still had a long way to go on the inside.

We all hope to be recognized for the person we are inside instead of who we appear to be externally. So let's not hide our real self but rather set it free.

Remember, things could be worse
All you have to do is look at the newspaper to read sad heart wrenching stories of others who are in worse straights than you. Unfortunates who have lost their homes or loved ones to some tragedy, who have been without work for years despite their superhuman efforts, who are victims of natural disasters that just seem to be increasing in ferocity and frequency, or those who commit horrendous acts of violence because they have lost any semblance of humanity or empathy. In the

case of the elderly it is just as bad as stories of senility and loss of independence and scams targeting seniors frequently make the headlines.

Yes you are getting older and yes it is not easy and yes there are challenges that at times seem insurmountable. But in most cases things could be worse. You have made it this far so you know you are a fighter. Hang in there and stay the course as best you can.

Smile
Often times beyond our control a spontaneous smile hints at the happiness we feel within. Few people look more attractive than when they flash their pearly whites. And who would not rather engage a smiling person than a frowning one? Mark Twain said, *"Wrinkles should merely indicate where smiles have been."* Sometimes as we get older we forget the simple power a smile holds both for the person smiling as well as the recipient of the smile. Have you ever judged a senior citizen grumpy with a smile on their face? A smiling face means a happy person. And the wonderful thing about a smile is that even if you do not feel overly happy at that moment, when you put a grin on your face you start to feel better. Just give it a try next time you are in need of a little pick-me-up.

Focus on the positives in your life

I'm retired (and yes past the honeymoon period). And I'm loving it! Each day opens up new possibilities. I find myself becoming more able to insist on things I want rather than satisfying other's expectations. I find myself more inclined to be the family historian, telling the stories told to me, passing on the legacy of my life and my ancestor's lives to my grand kids. I don't necessarily need excitement, just newness. Don't do the same old stuff you always did. Try something new each day.

Aside from the physical aspects (I will miss my young legs), it can be helpful to look at the many positives that have come with our advancing years and the life experiences that made us into the people we are.

I have successfully raised two wonderful children who make me proud each time we interact. Each has grown into a young adult filled with those values that are important in life and critical to their continuing happiness. Had I not grown older (not OLD), I would not have been with them each step of the way helping where needed, encouraging on occasion, and admiring their progress often. I would not change it for the world.

With age can come wisdom. Friends and family may quickly point out that we have not nearly reached the pinnacle of our ultimate wisdom, but it's all good as long as we have been learning along the way. We will be headed down the right path if we learn not to sweat the little things but instead accept that not everything will go the way we want, nor necessarily should it. We will be on target once we have learned the immeasurable value of our family who have been with us through numerous difficult times, supported us, loved us, and without whom some of us would not be the people we are today (or maybe even here today). We will be making serious progress when we have learned that it is okay to cry because if we feel like crying, there is a reason. True wisdom will be within our grasp once we have learned that our spouse is our best friend, our confidant, consciously blind to our faults, always there when we need her. And we will be wise beyond our years once we have learned that money does not make the moment nor buy happiness – that can only be found within us. Wisdom can indeed come with age but it is up to each of us to nurture and help it grow.

Realize that frugal can be fun! Life can be enjoyed on a budget, economically. Extravagant spending does not proportionately increase pleasure. Finding a good deal is satisfying in itself and as long as you are with the one you love, every moment has the potential to be memory making.

Whatever our age, it is can help to realize we cannot change the past, we do not know what the future holds and so our best bet is to live in this present moment. We should take aim to focus on today, now and live it fully. It is all about how we choose to view the world and the attitude with which we face our future. Accepting our aging is just part of the journey.

Chapter 5 - Preparing Relationships for Retirement

Grow old with me! The best is yet to be. ~ Robert Browning

Chances are that when you move into retirement you will be sharing your life with another. Whether you have been together for a long time or only an abbreviated period, the two of you will cross into the post working world together. And that is typically how we envision it. We look forward to sharing more time together, exploring new interests together, and enjoying more of just the two of us than was possible while we were pulled in sometimes conflicting directions by our careers and commitments. There is so much to do when we have the time to do it and who better to do it with than our significant other. Together we have been through good times and bad, happiness and sadness, bumps in the road both big and small, and somehow managed to survive with most of our marbles intact. Best of all, with our dues paid we are now free to get to know each other all over again. We can concentrate on the two of us like when we first started out. Retirement is our time to put aside the stresses of the working world and responsibilities of raising a family to focus 100 percent on doing what makes us both happy.

During your pre-retirement lives, each of you are likely engaged in respective careers. Typically the job occupied the majority of time with Monday to Friday dedicated to work. Within those careers you established a certain persona best equipped to succeed in your role. Years of experience and training combined to make you into the highly effective employee that you were on the job.

At the same time, outside of work existed a second persona focused on your family and friends, your interests and passions, and those activities that fill your time when unplugged from the job. If you were to look back at how you divided time between these two priorities a 50-50 split would probably not be very accurate. More likely you spent a majority of your time – for some a significant majority – focused on the work side of things. But for that time in your life and given our current hyper competitive world, such dedication was necessary and generally accepted behavior. Now in retirement you need no longer divide your time or share your focus. Free of work encumbrances the person you are outside of work assumes center stage.

The challenge for some can be after so many years focused on the job, your personality away from work may remain somewhat underdeveloped. You were really good at what you did but when no longer doing it may find yourself unable to easily flip the switch and assume your non-working persona. And unfortunately for all involved those traits and characteristics so important to your career success do not always translate well outside of the business environment. But do not despair – you now have time to become who you want to be going forward. And you have your spouse, with a vested interest for sure, ready at your side to help get to where you want to go. Adjustments and changes for the better will benefit both partners as each evolves into a role in retirement that no longer includes a full time job. Finding that balance and achieving that harmony within your newly joined 24/7 relationship can help keep your retirement fresh and on the right track.

George Elliot said, *"What greater thing is there for human souls than to feel that they are joined for life – to be with each other in silent unspeakable memories."* Inspirational words for couples who have shared happy memories and are generally in sync, looking forward to their retirement life at each other's side. However, there are couples who after pursuing individual paths in career and life may experience a disconnection from their partner when retirement arrives. Their main focus over the years has been individual. Now with the specter of retirement hovering they realize they do not really know their partner. Each is very good at pursuing their individual interests but not so much together. Sure they have spent time together to some extent, but they may find they are quite unprepared to exist side by side 24/7.

For these momentarily distanced couples retirement can be a time to reconnect and come together. With time on their hands and no career distractions they have the chance to get to know each other all over again. The time is right to re-learn what makes the partner tick, what drives their passion, what feeds their fear, and most importantly how the two are going to share a fulfilling retirement life. If all goes well, they can count on living many more years with one another. Getting retirement off to a good start as soon as possible will only add to the satisfaction those years can provide.

Timing is everything

What matters most is I don't want to spend my life working and working and working. I have the most difficult time letting go. My husband is retired and enjoys every minute of every day. He wants me to spend more time with him. Why is it so difficult to give up a career? By the way I am a successful, self-employed business woman but at the end of your life, who cares if you did not spend it with your family.

It is not always the case that both parties retire at the same time. More typically one departs the working world while the other remains employed for a to-be-determined length of time. This can be a good thing for a number of reasons. The employed partner continues to receive insurance coverage for both of you, an increasingly expensive proposition. Once neither of you is employed the premiums and fees will become entirely your responsibility. Depending on your financial situation some portion of the income earned can continue to go directly into your retirement fund via 401k or IRA or other investment plans. Even if you are satisfied with the size of your retirement nest egg, adding to it while you can is a good idea. And depending on the difference in ages you may choose to stagger your retirement dates to better coincide with Social Security payments and assure you receive the maximum benefits.

One of you may want to get an early jump start on the whole retirement experience. Instead of simultaneously committing whole hog the first retired can begin to navigate the retirement jungle and start to experience firsthand the post working world. In these early days he or she can begin to understand just how accurate you have been in your estimation of what retired life will be. Are the activities you have planned sufficient to keep you engaged and excited? How difficult is it to adapt to this new world where what you do is entirely in your own control? Were your estimates of expenses an accurate reflection of reality? Were your expectations realistic?

After careful thought and planning some decide the best solution is to go ahead and jump into their second act at the same time. Together you can explore all that retirement has to offer. Through trial and error you can find what works best in your situation. Where adjustments need to be made, you do so. And when you discover some aspect of being retired that absolutely excites and ignites both of you, you are there to share and enjoy it together.

Understand your individual views of retirement
Before you retire it can be helpful and quite enlightening to discuss how you each see retirement life unfolding. You have been together for awhile and know a lot about the person you are with. But your observations are of a working person who you see only half of the time. What should you expect from a full time fellow retiree at your side? What do they expect from you?

You might begin the discussion by each describing your vision of the perfect retirement. Do you picture yourself sitting on the deck as the sun goes down with a nice glass of wine in your hand relaxing in the knowledge that you do not have to be doing anything at that moment? Are you happiest doing less rather than attempting to cram every minute full of activity? Do you revel in silence and seek a peaceful alternative to the hectic pace of the working world?

Or are you someone who thrives best in a state of perpetual motion, always needing to do something while simultaneously planning what you will do next? Do you constantly need new experiences to make your day meaningful? Do you view retirement as your chance to do everything you never could and plan to attack that bucket list with a vengeance?

You can see there might be challenges should a couple hold widely divergent views of an ideal retirement life. It is helpful to understand what each desire, where you have common interests and where you diverge.

I think that each and every person and each and every couple should sit down and make a list of what they want, need and expect in retirement. Some couples might find they are not on the same page in how they want to spend retirement years. In order to attain a goal you have to define it and plan for it. These things don't just magically happen once you start retirement.

Assuming this is your first time retiring, you may not know exactly what to expect. You may find yourself unsure of how your plans to live your second act coincide or conflict with your partner. Here are a few topics worthy of discussion as you attempt to map your course:

Do you picture retirement as a time to relax from your busy life or a time to do all you can do? Obviously your life can include a combination but at a high level do think you lean one way or the other?

What is most important to each of you in retirement? What does your partner most want to do? Think about your goals, fun activities, aspirations, and inner motivations.

How long do you expect your retirement life to last? It is one thing to prepare for the next five to ten years but what about the next twenty to thirty?

Do you think you might return to work of some kind in retirement? Or do you hope to never work again?

Create individual bucket lists and then compare the results. There is nothing wrong with pursuing individual dreams but it would also be nice to know interests that you have in common.

Are there any specific things that each of you want to accomplish in retirement?

What activities do you see yourself engaged in? Not what you have to do but what you want to do.

Are there things you definitely want to avoid in retirement?

Which of your skills do you most enjoy using? How might you apply those in your retired life?

If you are able to uncover each other's perspectives of what will make for a fulfilling retirement, you might better understand each other's motivations before the two of you begin your journey.

Identify shared and individual interests

One retirement surprise was that my wife and I could not only coexist but actually have our relationship strengthened by being together 24/7. We are both independent people. There was uneasiness that having no break from each other would be quite difficult. That has not happened. In fact, just the opposite.

I look forward to sharing time and many adventures with my wife when we finally retire together. There is so much to do and no one I would rather do it with than her. We both love to travel and once the work schedule no longer dictates our life we will be off into the wild blue yonder! With the freedom to act spur of the moment we will be able to take advantage of those mid-week specials where not only is the cost less but so are the crowds. And who knows, we might even look into the RV world and the possibility of driving off into the sunset together. Honestly I believe we talk about our travels-to-be every day as we imagine just how glorious it will be.

It is important that a couple shares similar interests when they retire. I mean if you had nothing in common you would probably not be together, right? And now that you control how you spend your time, it becomes even more important otherwise those days together may start to feel pretty long. Looking at the incredibly busy schedule my parents maintain I quickly see that their common interests have kept them entertained and active for many years. You know they are busy when you need a magnifying glass to read the small print on the calendar due to the sheer number of things planned. The interests they share include bridge, tennis, theatre, wine tasting, the symphony, travel near and far, family events, and dinner parties with friends and family. No moss gathers on their heels and although the pace may be extreme for me, it works for the two of them and that's what it's all about. Being interested in similar activities is an important part of a successful shared retirement.

In addition to common interests it is equally important to maintain our own individual pursuits. When we retire we will be at each other's side 24/7. We wake together, eat together, spend the day together, spend the night together and then do it all again. If we really want to enjoy that shared time, I think it is important that we allow time for ourselves as well. Face it, not everything that interests me has the same attraction for my wife. However, it is healthy for us each to pursue those passions that are not mutually shared. And it is healthy for both parties to allow and encourage this time apart. Back to my folks, in addition to shared interests my dad likes golf and my mom encourages him to play as often as he likes. Not only does it entertain dad but it gives mom time to do her own thing. Where dad has golf and playing the trumpet, mom has her ladies bridge and women's tennis. When they get back together they have a fresh outlook and new stories to tell.

Retirees to be can benefit from a better understanding of areas of mutual as well as divergent interests. Maintaining broader interests can make us more interesting and fun to be with. The trick is to try to create a balance between shared and individual interests. Maybe if we give and take a little we can live and love a little more.

Who will be responsible for what?
Typically during working careers you each did whatever needed to be done around the house when you had the time to do it. If a carpet needed vacuuming or a lawn needed mowing, if a load of clothes was building up or the cat needed to go to the vet, whoever had the time would step up and handle it. Once you retire both of you will have time on your hands. You can keep things running more smoothly if you divide responsibilities to some extent. It is only fair that if one of you cooks the dinner the other cleans up the dishes. You share the living arrangement so share the chores. If you really hate one particular chore negotiate (my wife hates vacuuming and I do not mind; I prefer eating rather than cooking a meal and she is a great and willing cook). It is not necessary to dole out every little responsibility. But it can help if there is an agreement as to who does what for the bigger concerns.

Most couples maintain a shared bank account but some also have their individual accounts. If you have not already done so prior to retiring you may want to discuss and agree upon who will handle what bills. Some expenses fall in the realm of the shared account while others can become the responsibility of one or the other of you. Once again, a little clarity can go a long way.

Retirement fears
We all want to optimistically focus on the positive and exciting promise of retirement living. But it does not hurt to discuss fears that might be harbored as well. You are in this together for better or worse and the fewer surprises along the way the better.

As you age you will face inevitable physical and mental challenges. The reality is over time we will become less independent. Basic acts that we took for granted while younger may likely become more difficult. Remembering simple things is no longer guaranteed. It is a scary state of affairs but cannot be ignored. It can be helpful if couples discuss honestly and openly their fears regarding aging. If you have a family history of health issues you should share details with your spouse. Open communication can help all concerned.

The list of possible fears associated with retirement and aging can be long. Some can refuse to worry while others attempt to ignore them and hope for the best. Rather than burying our heads in the sand it can be useful to address what scares us up front. We have our ever loving partner to help us along the way so long as they know where to pitch in.

Family and Friends

When I was young, I hated it when my dad tried to impart his wisdom to me because he was "older and wiser." Looking back, I see he was right about pretty much everything he told me. He claimed he could look at a situation and see down the road how it would turn out, just by relying on his life experiences. I didn't think that was possible back then. But I do now.

In addition to the relationship with our partner, we may want to prepare for our interaction with family and friends as we enter retirement. With more time on our hands the opportunity exists to re-engage those with whom we have fallen out of touch should we so desire. Old schoolmates, friends from our childhood, co-workers who we enjoyed engaging with but lost contact, all await our outreach. With today's social media tools it is almost impossible for someone to hide should we set our mind to finding them. And don't forget family members near and far who might love to reinsert themselves into our lives now that there is more time and less distraction.

Before you know it, you may find yourself busily engaged with regular lunch appointments and meetings over coffee, with dinner dates and unexpected phone calls as those who were not an active part of your busy work life now vie for your attention. It can be a wonderful exciting time as you rekindle lost relationships and bring each other up to speed with all that has happened since your last interactions.

So, you retired to get away from all the hustle and bustle of the working world to give yourself time to pursue what you are most interested in. Now you discover you have become a social butterfly with few openings on your busy calendar. Is this really what you wanted? If it is, more power to you. Enjoy your time sharing and celebrate your retirement.

But it is possible that this is not quite what you had in mind as you dreamed of retirement. Maybe you enjoy a bit of social interaction but have your limits. Perhaps you love your family dearly but small doses work best for all concerned. And what about that special time you were planning to set aside for you to explore your second act? Should it come to be that you find yourself overcommitted, it is up to you to manage your time as well as the expectations of friends and family. It is important to balance time with others and time alone. Both are essential to a happy retirement attitude but you need to adjust the mix to fit your own personal preference. Before it gets out of hand, you may want to consider the different possible courses, consider how each will impact your retirement and try to do what is best for you.

Sharing your time

Once retired you have more time available to spend with friends and family. Relationships that have been left idle can be rekindled. Relatives who you have not spent enough time with over the years can be reintroduced into your life. You can even dig up old classmates from high school or earlier if you are so inclined. But before you go too crazy, you might take a minute to think about what you are doing.

For a relationship to work both parties should get something from it. If you find yourself always on the giving side, always making concessions, always doing what the other wants regardless of your wishes, how healthy is the relationship? How sustainable is such a one-sided friendship? And ultimately how much work and effort do you really want to put into maintaining it? Time is a precious commodity even in retired life.

There are times in a relationship when you will naturally give more than you get back. Friends are there to help each other – that is why it is called friendship. But if the scale is tipped perpetually in one direction, it can be a losing proposition. At such times it is up to you to make changes. If you do nothing, that valuable time you worked so hard to realize in retirement might go up in smoke.

Babysitting services

A perfect love sometimes does not come until the first grandchild. ~ Welsh Proverb

Is there anything more wonderful than grandchildren? Beautiful little chips-off-the-old-block packed with energy and excitement capable of bringing spontaneous smiles to your face. They can truly be a joy to behold and talk about feelings of pride! Some retirees cannot get enough of their grandchildren and want to see them all the time. And what grandchild would not want to be spoiled endlessly by their doting grandparents? The relationship between grandparents and grandchildren can be incredibly strong with both sides receiving heaps of love while creating glorious memories.

And as a grandparent one equally wonderful moment can be at the end of the day when your kids and their kids head home. A good time has been had by all and everyone is happy and tired. Now they return to their lives and you can get back to the life you know. On the next visit the slate is clean, imaginations rekindled and energy levels restored.

My wife and I are not that far from potentially becoming grandparents and it is exciting. We joke about the joy of playing with the little ones and when the diapers need changing calling in the parents. After all it is their kid! We joke about it but actually do not have a problem with changing diapers. But there is a hint of truth in our humor. While we look forward to spending time with our grandchildren-to-be, we do not want to be seen as a babysitting service. Of course we plan to help out when needed and maybe even watch them overnight on occasion. But we have raised our kids and now have the time and remaining sanity to be together, to travel, to enjoy a quiet evening free of distraction that we do not introduce. We plan to make it clear that while we love our grandchildren, while we love spending time with them and their parents, at the end of the day we are free birds who need to spread our wings and fly. At least that is the plan. Who knows if we will be so steadfast in our convictions when the little gremlins actually arrive on the scene?

Your relationship with You

As a good retiree to be, you are doing due diligence as you consider and plan how to best integrate your life with that of your spouse so as to complement each other in retirement. And you have contemplated how to effectively divide and share your time with friends and family to address potential issues before they occur. It is a wonderful thing you are doing and before too long you will appreciate your time and effort spent. But don't overlook that other important relationship you need to maintain in retirement, namely your relationship with you.

No one knows you better than you know yourself. There is no other person on earth who can see as clearly into your passions and motivations or better understand your fears and hopes. If you have been fortunate enough during your career and raising a family to set aside some personal time for reflection, you are to be congratulated. Many are so caught up in every day emergencies and distractions that they are unable to escape to any quality time alone. Yet it is sometimes during time spent one on one with yourself that you are most able to gain a deeper understanding into your life, its challenges and your direction. It is when you can finally step off the treadmill and catch your breath for a moment that you can gain clearer insight into your future and what you can do to experience a meaningful existence. Without time to think through a situation and weigh possible outcomes you can find yourself taking action based on incomplete information in a knee jerk fashion.

Now you are about to retire. You will soon be able to step back from the hurried lifestyle you have come to accept as normal. This is the perfect opportunity to pause, slow your thought process, and think through those important aspects of your life to be. It is up to you to assure that along with the attention you lavish on family and friends you set aside quality time for yourself. Time to do whatever brings you happiness whether that be swinging in a hammock or climbing a distant peak or singing a song or writing a book.

As you take some time for you, try not to be overly self critical. No one on the planet expects you to be perfect so don't mistakenly set your own standards too high. Yes, you have made mistakes in the past but you cannot change them now. The future is what you will make of it so do away with guilt and remorse over what could have been. Cut yourself some slack and use this time to take steps to make yourself a better happier person. You will hopefully live many years in your retirement so learn to be a friend and ally to yourself.

Now is a good time to be either happy with who you are or make some changes. It has taken you 65 or so years to evolve into the person you are today. All of your personal experiences, the world and environment you grew up in and the influence of those around you blend together to create the unique individual that is you. Think back on the positive things you have done and remember how good it made you feel. Now is your chance to feel that way again as often as you want.

How do others view you? Do you believe that you are seen in a positive way by family and friends? Or do you feel that you are thought badly of? And how much does it really matter? Consider how important it is in your life what others think of you.

If it is very important then it is up to you to make changes where necessary. If it is not important then you can go about your life secure in the knowledge that you are happy with who you are.

Are there areas you could be better? There are always areas where you could be better. But how important is it to you to make those changes to the person you are? What will be the long term impact on your quality of retired life if you do nothing to address your perceived shortcomings? If you truly believe that modifying some part of your personality will enhance your life going forward, now is the time to do something about it. Do what you can to fix it so you can focus on enjoying yourself. If you are content with you as is, if you accept the good and the bad and the ugly, enjoy the moment and live your happy life.

Chapter 6 – Choosing to Work in Retirement

It is the working man who is the happy man.
It is the idle man who is the miserable man.
~ Benjamin Franklin

By the time we reach retirement age most of us will have worked for more than forty years in our chosen career or as if often the case multiple careers. When it is all said and done over half of our life will have been spent diligently performing our duty as members of the working world. We are all too familiar with the dreaded Monday morning start of a new week when we drag ourselves out of bed whether we want to or not because the job is calling, because we have responsibilities, because this is what we must do. Although some view their job positively and even find enjoyment in what they do, for most of us it is a means to an end with the promise of a paycheck the main motivation keeping us at it.

As current members of the rat race, we have been conditioned to live for Friday and the idyllic life to be rediscovered over our short weekend escape. Unfortunately how often do we find that Saturday rolls around with that list of things to do and hobbies to pursue but we find our self just too darn tired to get it done? How many times did "the job" suck all of the drive and passion right out, leaving us in a weekend survival and recovery mode instead of a what-will-I-do-for-fun mode? And have you ever fantasized how wonderful it would be to reverse the accepted order of things to work two days and enjoy a weekend that is five glorious days long? But of course that is not the American way where the fulltime work year posits a minimum 2080 hours of work with career aspirations often driving us well beyond that threshold.

Should we be fortunate enough to survive our employment adventure and ultimately arrive at our time to retire, we hope at long last to be free to happily exit the working world and enter into a new chapter in our lives. It is here that we will finally have the opportunity to pursue those many interests that we could not while trapped within our job. We will have the time to take it down a notch, to slow the pace to a more desirable level, to smell the roses and patiently watch the grass grow. Or if we prefer we might busily engage in exotic travel and challenging projects, in exciting adventures and stimulating new experiences, in meaningful efforts across diverse areas that we would never have thought of while immersed in our role as worker bee. The world is our oyster and the opportunity is now.

This new found freedom can be invigorating with all its freshness and possibility but it does not come without its own set of challenges. Yes I am now free to do those things that I want to, living outside of any formal organized routine or schedule. I am now responsible for my future. It is up to me to choose what I want to do and then to do it. My calendar of things to do can be as busy or as barren as I choose to make it. Routine need never enter my day so long as I can come up with fresh activities and new interests to keep me engaged. But if I have not been looking ahead to retirement, if I have no real idea of what I will do for those many years of freedom ahead, what exactly am I going to do?

I am past retirement age and still employed and have no plans to slow down. I find the young people don't understand the elderly and there are a lot of misconceptions. I am in better health and feel great. I love changes and many challenges and my brain is at 200 percent capacity!

Many of us would like to think ourselves spontaneous and capable of filling our retirement dance card with an endless variety of enjoyable activities and adventures. But have we really taken the time to figure out exactly what that means? Have we honestly thought about what we will do for the next twenty or thirty years when there is no one telling us what to do? The scary reality is that some retirees to be spend more time planning for a week's vacation than for the many years of retired living they have in store.

When it comes to considering if there is a place for work in your retirement there are two main camps – those who must work and those who have the option to work if they want to. The first is generally made up of people who must work due to their financial situation or other concerns. Some may enter retirement full of expectations of good times to be only to discover that they are unable to pay their bills and live the lifestyle they want solely on their current investments and savings. Others may have been forced from the workforce prematurely due to a company reorganization or downsizing, denied sufficient time to save as they had planned to provide for their retirement. Although they may wish they could retire the reality is they have no option but to continue working if they can find and keep a job. And there is no guarantee that the willing and able 55 year old in search of employment will be able to find and keep a reasonable job. Although older workers may be less likely to lose their jobs than younger counterparts, those older job seekers will typically search longer for their next gig. By 2011 the median duration of unemployment for those over 55 was 35 weeks while younger workers were successful at landing a job on average within 26 weeks. (5) We have all seen the elderly man or woman working at Wal-Mart or Walgreens earning whatever money they can to help make ends meet. Some may be there by choice but many have no other place to go. It is a truly scary situation that is unfortunately increasingly common as seniors deal with recent turmoil in the economy, housing market and rising healthcare costs.

Things don't always go as planned. Over the years I have had three major job changes with some time unemployed between each and as a result a secure retirement has been delayed. My advice is to control debt during times of difficulty. I have been fortunate to be able to continue working fulltime well past 65. Now the road ahead looks a little brighter.

If you are middle age or beyond and forced to find a job, what can you do to increase your odds of being hired? A few years back at 52 year of age I found myself out of a job due to the purchase of my company. It took me over a year and a half to find my next gig and in less than one year that company was acquired and my responsibilities moved to the East coast corporate office. So once again I find myself engaged in the joys of job searching only this time at age 54. As one who has been searching for my next job for over a year now, I believe have learned a thing or two that might help my fellow middle agers trying to get back on track. (NOTE: if you are not currently in search of a job, you may want to skip these tips and move on to page 60 where we look at why you may still wish to consider work even though you do not need to.)

Leverage your co-workers, friends and family
Many jobs are never officially advertised. Instead the hiring manager lets it be known she needs to fill a particular position and the request is circulated within the company among its employees. These days everyone knows someone who is looking for a job and many times their

experience matches the requirements for the job. If you let your network know you are looking and describe what you are looking for, they may be able to help. As part of your search consider taking someone to lunch or coffee every day, reach out to old contacts from previous jobs, and be sure to update your online information so if someone checks you out they get a powerful first impression. The more people that know you are looking the better your chances that someone somewhere may have an in.

Stay current on technology
Living in the Bay Area as I do it is paramount to stay current with the latest technologies and trends if I hope to have any chance at a viable job. Hiring managers are often younger with track records in the months and years rather than decades. They know all about the latest and greatest social media tools and talk the current buzz. If all of the other candidates for the job have this capability you must as well. Set up a Facebook account and see what it is all about. Sign up for Twitter and tweet a bit. Look into the world of blogs to see how opinions are influenced. Try to think like the younger generation who goes to the web to search for everything from the nearest coffee shops to movie times to the best route to destinations based on current traffic conditions. You will never see anyone younger than 30 looking at a paper map to plot their course. Immerse yourself in the technology of this generation if you hope to keep up.

Even at the age of 70 I find that staying up with current trends in connectivity is important. My children and grandchildren are always connected. I simply follow them on FourSquare or where ever they happen to be online this week. They really don't want to talk nor do they seem to have the time so text messaging is the mode we use.

But don't get too comfortable. This media is evolving everyday and what works today will be outdated within a few months. I have learned to accept it and can adapt in a heartbeat.

Have your elevator pitch ready

As you engage in your search you will be asked to highlight what it is that you have done over the years as well as what it is you are looking for in your next job. This is your chance to clearly and succinctly paint a picture of your major accomplishments and successes. Don't overdo it but don't forget you are selling yourself and your skills. In the sales world from which I evolved it is important to list specific examples with numbers where possible. For example I achieved 130 percent of quota for the five years while at company "X" or I closed the biggest single deal in the history of the company or similar factoids. Practice your lines so you can recite them cold. Your story should come off as natural not rehearsed. Continue to fine tune and improve the message over time to get it just right. I typically recite my mantra in the car or while walking around the block until it sounds natural.

You will also want to develop your pitch for the kind of job you would like to land. You can think of this as your chance to create the job description of your ideal job. Depending how long you have been searching the description may be specific or broader. Focus on those things you would enjoy doing as you outline what you want in your next job.

Be your own recruiter
Recruiters typically charge between 10-30 percent of your first year salary to place you in a job. This can be a significant amount especially for higher level positions as are more typical with senior job searchers. The good ones typically have connections across the industry and are sometimes privy to jobs before they become public knowledge so it makes good sense to work with those you know and trust. But why not become your own recruiter? You know what it is that you want to be doing, what you like doing and what you are most skilled at doing. Take that information and begin your search for companies that fit your sweet spot.

You can start with the company website. Go to the About link or the Company link on the site to find a Careers section that shows you what positions are currently available. See if any of the advertised positions are your cup of tea. Even if there is nothing that fits your specific requirements you will find contact information for the human resources folks. Typically you will find something like jobs@company or careers@company. Generally there is a main phone number as well. You can also find the names of current executives under the Management Team section. Now you can get started.

Create a cover letter that is unique to grab the attention of the HR team who likely wades through hundreds each week. The letter should be brief and you want to make your impact in the first paragraph or two. If possible make specific reference to a past accomplishment that would be applicable to the position you seek to demonstrate your worth. Don't talk about what you can do but rather give examples of what you have successfully done in past roles. People looking for a job will say they "will do" whatever it takes but if you can give real examples of where you "have done" your story is more credible.

Send the cover letter into the HR department or directly to the executive in charge of the department. You can figure out the email syntax by looking at examples on their website. Some typical combinations include:
 <firstname><lastname>@<company>.com,
<firstinitial><lastname>@<company>.com, or
<firstname>@<company>.com. If you decide to "go high" and target the executive contact you will in most cases be routed down to the HR team

anyway. But if that executive takes even a moment to read the first paragraph, you have a chance to pique their interest.

You will generally want to follow up on the phone as well as email to set yourself above the rest of the interested job seekers. Know what you are going to say, be succinct and to the point, and sell them on what you have to offer. And be confident. If you have identified a good match between your skill set and what the company does, you know you can be a benefit to them. And don't forget there is no 10-30 percent fee to bring you on board.

Stay engaged while you search
If you have been out of work for an extended period of time you can bet that one of the questions you will be asked during an interview is "what have you been doing with your time?" If all you can come up with is searching for a job, you are missing an opportunity to impress. You are selling yourself as an excited, energetic, go-getter always looking for your next challenge. Such a person would surely take advantage of available time to improve their skills or advance their interests. Taking a class in something that compliments your job is always a good choice as you show commitment to improving yourself. But I think there is also value in any project or serious undertaking that you pursue. For example, what if while you are between jobs you became an amateur photographer after attending classes and

completing your master portfolio? You have taken the initiative to do something new, you show your ability to stick to it by completing your courses and portfolio, you demonstrate that you are not afraid of change, and you reinforce your claim that you are not one to waste valuable time. When I found myself unemployed for an extended period I did not want to attend classes but had always been interested in writing. So I set out on a project to build a website and create a blog. Not only did this allow me to showcase my evolving writing skills but I also became engaged in the world of blogging and social media far beyond what I would have learned in books or classes. I even went so far as to eventually self-publish my first book. Now when I am asked what I did outside of my job search I can share the passion and excitement I experienced writing and publishing a book. All I need is the right interview!

You only make one first impression

Although the truth is beauty is more than skin deep, your appearance at the interview is going to make some impression on the interviewer. It is up to you to make that as positive an impression as possible. Do not wear outdated suites or dresses. That plaid three-piece-suit from college is not likely to ever come back into style. Make sure your shoes are stylish and shined. Wear a haircut or style that is fashionable. If you want to hide some of the gray, check into coloring your hair. Just be sure that the color is somewhere in the palette of genuine believable hair color. Older folks can on occasion have some redness to their eyes – nothing that a little Visine cannot fix. When you shake hands do so with a firm grip and be sure your hand is dry. A limp sweaty handshake is not the way you want to begin your interview. Make eye contact during the process but don't stare like a zombie. Speak in a clear measured voice, not too fast and not too slow. Be confident but not cocky. Remember through it all that you have done your research and the skills you bring to the table are a good fit for the position offered. Believe that you can do the job and do it well. You just need the opportunity.

Be the best prepared candidate

Everyone spends some time preparing for their interview but if you want to rise above the crowd, try to be the best prepared. Take your time to learn all you can about the company, its management and its offerings. Watch the videos on the website, read the news releases to be up on current events, and check out executives on LinkedIn. Research the competition and know the industry. Prepare well thought out questions, the kind that shows you have more than just a cursory understanding. If you will meet with multiple interviewers, research each and have questions specific to their role at the company. Practice saying in your head the top 3-5 facts that set this company above the competition and talk about "our" company rather than your company. Have answers for those standard interview questions that tend to pop up such as "what is it about this company that has you interested" or "what will you bring to the company" or "why should we hire you". Prepare for the unexpected and you will impress their socks off.

Have the right attitude

Hiring managers are going to see a middle aged person when you walk through the door and the harsh reality is that they may subconsciously associate certain behaviors due to your age. You do not want to leave the interview with any of those misperceptions remaining. Try to be confident and energetic conveying an excitement about the company and your opportunity to work there. Give examples of how you have adapted to change in the past so you are not viewed as set in your ways. Give examples of learning new technologies or implementing new processes to show you not afraid of change. Describe situations when you solved problems, improved efficiencies, boosted morale, or received special recognition. Believe that you are good enough for this job. Be optimistic but not cocky.

If you are a member of the more fortunate second group that upon reaching retirement does not have to find a job, you still may want to consider if there is a place for work in your future. There are those who find true enjoyment in the careers they pursue. The work they do inspires them and challenges them and rewards them in a consistent way that life outside the job is not always capable of doing. These folks truly find passion in the work they do.

I seem to wander back and forth between part-time and full-time retirement. Every once in awhile a former client calls me up and I then get busy with either a brief or few-month-long consulting assignment. It generally turns out to be a good mix – largely because I appreciate the intellectual challenge.

Ask yourself if there might be some value or personal satisfaction in pursuing work beyond retirement. Remember that the responsibility to create an engaging fulfilling second act rests squarely on your shoulders. You should consider all possible avenues as you build your retirement map. Is it reasonable to suggest that there might be a certain benefit, a positive aspect about being a member of the working masses where days are typically chocked full of things to do? Could the satisfaction we get interacting with co-workers be something we want to sustain as a part of our retirement solution? Would retirement be more fulfilling if we continued to participate in a company culture and environment?

As we prepare for our extended retirement life, it can be helpful to consider the role work might play whether by choice or due to necessity. If you are blessed to have the freedom to choose, would you want to work in retirement or not? To help in your decision process, let's take a look at some of the pluses and the minuses associated with working in retirement.

The Pluses

All I ever wanted to do in life was to make a difference in the lives of others. Each and every day in some way, big or small, my profession allows me to do that. When I read about individuals who can't wait to leave their lifelong profession and retire to something meaningful, it only serves to remind me how fortunate I have been.

Interaction with others

Most of us are social animals. We do better and are generally happier when we interact with others. And the work environment is one place where interaction is at a premium. Here we combine our skills with those of others in such a way that the sum of our efforts is greater than our individual contributions. We adapt, compromise and learn how to get along with each other in as well as outside of the work environment. By sharing in successes we achieve harmony and experience satisfaction from a job well done. Even our failures can be of value if we continue to improve and learn to accept we are not perfect. On the worksite we share the struggle, experience the humor, learn from each other and interact on a regular basis. There are some who will never be as close to anyone as they are to fellow workers on the job.

Best of all is the just plain fun side as we meet around the coffee machine to share tales of the recent weekend, brag about the accomplishments of our children, and update each other on the latest gossip. How we enjoy those moments interspersed throughout the day when we share a bit of ourselves with our co-workers. Watching each other grow and mature and succeed in our careers can be inspiring and heartwarming, especially when we look back to earlier days where the journey was just beginning. All said it should be no surprise that one of the main reasons seniors return to the workforce is to engage with others.

A place to go with something to do each day

Yes we are all creative individuals but are we creative enough to fill our many retirement days with purposeful activities that stimulate our lives? One of my biggest retirement fears is running out of meaningful things to do each day. The successful retirement life I envision is not just about keeping busy to fill the hours. I want to be able to look back at the end of the day to see that my time was well spent, that I accomplished something worthwhile. I want to make the most of my time not fritter it away. Of course not every day will need to be entirely productive. I plan to watch my fair share of grass growing and flowers blooming, of sunsets slowly running their course, of people milling about the mall or neighborhood park going about their lives. In other words just chilling and going with the flow. However a lifetime of days spent in such a manner is not going to cut it for me or for many retirees.

When we are working, our daily activities are laid out ahead of time. We need not rely strictly upon our own creativity to fill in the blanks. Having a schedule can create a certain feeling of security. Everything is taken care of – we just show up and get to it. Now if the job we are talking about is boring by its nature or stifling to our creativity or otherwise disagreeable, then perhaps that feeling of security can be better experienced elsewhere. But for the right situation, a job in retirement can offer a predictable, consistent, active day filled with something worthwhile to do.

Praise for a job well done
Most of us are familiar with setting and chasing goals from a work, sport or personal perspective. It is ingrained in us since toddlers that if we want to get something done we better set goals. From our work environment our success or failure at the job is often measured by our progress against these targets. The impact can be negative when unrealistic goals are set with little or no hope of being reached. But on the positive side, upon completion of our goals we hope to receive recognition for a job well done. Whether this is in the form of a bonus, award, or some form of public praise, it just plain feels good. As a matter of fact for some this recognition can be one of the more important reasons they go to work. Money aside,

the recognition for their effort can add meaning to their world. Outside of work you cannot count on your extra efforts necessarily being recognized or acknowledged in any consistent manner.

Opportunity to explore a whole new career
The type of work we choose to pursue in retirement does not necessarily need to be like anything we have done before. Encore careers can offer the chance to try something new and experiment with areas previously untested. As you plan for retirement, think back to what you dreamed of being when you were young. Before the realities of bills and family and responsibilities influenced your career path, what was it you most wanted to do when you grew up? Retirement could be your chance to take a stab at it. Of course at 65 you are probably not qualified to be a fireman or ballerina and maybe an astronaut is a bit out of reach. But there are still a lot of things you are capable of doing and now you finally have the time to do so.

If going all the way back to youthful times for inspiration is asking too much, what about those possibilities and dreams that popped into your head over the course of your career? What about those intriguing technologies or exciting new companies that you learned of along the way? Retirement can be your time to take a chance on something new. If money is not the driving factor you might get started by offering your services at affordable rates or even free to begin with. The trick is to get in the door and give it a try. If it does not work out you can move on. But what if it does?

Finally what about those ideas for your own business you may have contemplated over the years? Imagine doing your own thing with you as the boss, working hours that best fit your style and optimum productivity, implementing creative ideas that you come up with, and building something from scratch. Seeing your baby grow from the ground up can be one of the most satisfying experiences you may realize. Home based businesses are numerous and easy to set up. Are you a writer at heart just waiting for a chance to express your creative thoughts? Does the possibility of consulting intrigue you? Do you know other like minded individuals at a similar stage in life looking to undertake a new venture? Age 65 is no longer considered by most to be the end of the road but rather a time for new beginnings. This next chapter in your life can be the perfect breeding ground for an exciting encore career.

Additional money
Let's not overlook the reality that if we continue working our bank account will continue to be positively impacted. If we have learned anything over these past tumultuous years it is there is no sure thing when it comes to financial security. So it is never a bad thing for money to continue to flow in rather than only pour out.

Those are a handful of reasons why it may sound good to at least consider the possible role of work in your retirement life. There are some excellent reasons why having a job in some form could add to the quality of your retired day. Now let's take a look at some of the not so positive aspects of the working world. Do you really want to have to live like this if you have the option to retire?

The Minuses

Required to be at work every day

While the organized, just-follow-the-schedule nature of a job can be a positive for some, others run in horror from the restrictions of an overly-orchestrated existence. Retirement is our time to step outside of the regime that was work and experience the freedom to walk our own individual walk down whatever path we so desire. How can I experience all that retired life has to offer if I am required to be in the office nine-to-five? If I don't have my freedom in retirement, what is the point? My creativity will only be truly realized if I have the freedom to experiment and explore what I want when I want. Nope, the reason I retired was to get away and I plan on staying as far away as possible.

Pressure to meet deadlines

I find the term deadline very appropriate – if you do not get the project done on time, you are dead. The good news is that most deadlines are reasonably set with sufficient time to get them done, right? I don't think so. More typical is the situation where there is not enough time and not enough resources but the project must be completed as scheduled. Get ready to work through lunch and dinner and don't expect any respite with the weekend. And at the end should you miraculously complete your assignment on time, you can safely bet that your next do or die chance to prove yourself is just around the corner. Of course if pressure is your thing this is music to your ears. But if you are like most sane retirees to be, escaping the constant pressure of deadlines can not only add to the quality of your life but to its longevity. One can only survive in a pressure cooker so long before something has to give.

Constant competition to rise fastest up the corporate ladder

Face it, in corporate America it's all about getting ahead. The success of one's career is too often measured by where you reside in the corporate hierarchy. A long career is not automatically deemed successful without a bit of upward mobility to show for the years. And along with the relentless effort to get ahead, you can find yourself subject to an ever present collection of poor behaviors including but not limited to back stabbing, ulterior motives, gossip, and the sad feeling that you cannot trust anyone. As a retiree, you will no longer need to struggle to climb the ladder to fame and fortune. Where you are now can be just find thank you. Do you really want to put yourself through all that again?

Endless, mindless, pointless meetings

You know the kind, made up of participants who contribute nothing of worth but have an opinion on everything and compete to assure they receive their allotted airtime. One of my pet peeves was always meetings held for meetings sake. Just because it is on the schedule does not require an actual meeting if there is nothing new or significant to convey. Meetings tend to be part of work for better or worse, usually for worse. If you have the choice why subject yourself needlessly?

Stifling individual creativity

Many corporations have gotten so big and successful because they supposedly know how to do things just right. Processes and procedures that have been carefully honed over the years guide you step by step through your day. Don't ask why just follow the leader. Not surprisingly the corporate way does not often leave wiggle room for much creativity. If you are an artist at heart you can quickly feel like a caged bird with little freedom to express yourself or fly to new heights. If you crave the opportunity to creatively participate, smaller companies may offer a lot more leeway.

Boring

As we said earlier there are those fortunate folk who find their jobs stimulating and enjoy what they do. But even in the best of circumstances there can be times when you become bored with your role and responsibilities. In a worse scenario you are bored more often than not. And unfortunately because you must do those things that make up your job you have no choice but to continue.

Commuting sucks

Need I say more? If you want to make yourself cry, take a minute to calculate how many hours you have spent in transit to and from your workplace. How many traffic jams and delays, construction detours and seas of red lights have you lived through? How many stressful heart pounding moments endured before you realized you just will not make it to your appointment on time? In the Bay Area it is not uncommon to have an hour or more commute each way every day. That adds up to 40 hours per month or the equivalent of one week on the road. Might you be able to find a better way to spend those precious hours?

The younger boss

If you are middle age plus or minus a few years and want to work in the technology industry, chances are darn good that you will be working for someone younger. Extremely well educated college graduates with creative minds and boundless drive are not just the CEOs and VPs of tomorrow, but of today as well. I have always felt that if you can learn from your boss no matter what her age you are in a good situation. And if your boss is the type who leads by example and believes that respect is earned not entitled, so much the better. But it can be tough when someone a third of your age with only a fraction of the years experience tells you how to do the job right despite your belief to the contrary. Is it worth it? Only you can decide.

Why would anyone choose to work more than they absolutely had to? For many, work has been a necessary evil endured because of the paycheck at the end of the day. Far from inspiring, the monotony of the job has often stultified our creativity and made us but another cog in the corporate machine. With little room for individual creativity our candle of inspiration can flicker and in the worst of cases is extinguished. Tomorrow will be just like today which was just like yesterday. If I am sixty five and have built a sufficient nest egg why on earth would I want to work one more day than I absolutely have to?

Ultimately the retirement you will live is a unique and very personal choice. No one is better qualified than you to create the outline of how your perfect retirement will look. No one else is exactly like you so none understand better what makes you tick, what inspires you, what makes you feel you are living a worthwhile life. If you feel that your retirement might be more satisfying and rewarding if it includes work, then feel free to consider it. If the opposite case is true, put yourself at ease and follow the path you choose.

Here are a few websites that may be useful should you be in the market for a job:

http://seniorjobbank.com   Employers interested in our audience can advertise to and attract talented, dedicated people over the age of 50. Many companies advertising are committed to hiring baby boomers and older workers as part of their hiring strategy and truly believe in the value of this talent pool.

http://seniors4hire.org   A nationwide online Career Center and the #1 place on the Internet for businesses that value a diverse workforce to actively recruit folks in the U.S. 50 and older including retirees and senior citizens looking for a job and/or other ways to earn money.

http://www.retirementjobs.com   Our goal is to identify companies most-suited to older workers and match them with active, productive, conscientious, mature adults seeking a job or project that matches their lifestyle. Whether you are here seeking to supplement your income, a new challenge, a way to get out and meet people, or another reason, welcome! We are working hard to make each of your visits here a positive one, and we know our work will never quite be done.

Chapter 7 - To your Good Health

Joy and temperance and repose, slam the door on the doctor's nose.
~ Henry Wadsworth Longfellow

I think it is reasonably safe to say that at this stage in our lives we have all been made well aware of the importance of doing those things that are healthy and good for us. With worldwide attention focused on the benefits of organic foods, vitamins, nutrition, weight consciousness and cardiovascular health, we would have to be living in a cave to not have tuned into the familiar song. Avoid too much of this and be sure to do at least "x" amount of that. Make sure your diet includes some "y" and don't even think of putting that into your body. It can be somewhat confusing but at a high level I think by now we get it. We know the basics of what we need to do to stay healthy. Of course what we choose to do with this information is a different matter.

While recently on vacation in Mexico my wife and I noticed something alarming. We had been coming to the same spot each year for many years but something seemed different this time. The average vacationer was easily 55 or older – nothing new there. But it seemed that a much greater percentage were overweight and not by just a little. We also noticed more of the older people moving slowly and struggling as they walked up from the beach toward their room. We could not help but compare with a trip to Switzerland some years ago where the old people – some very old – could be seen mixed amongst the younger generations as they up the nearest mountainside. Swiss women in their seventies had their hiking sticks in hand with chins pointed to the nearby peaks and if you walked too slowly in front of them they passed you by. We did not notice any of the locals overweight by more than a few pounds. It appeared the active lifestyle of these residents kept them fit and healthy well into their later years allowing them to enjoy their life to the fullest.

In defense of the non-Swiss we did meet a wonderful 89 year lady old while vacationing in Mexico who breathed a little hope into all of us not-quite-yet-there in years. Throughout the week, she remained in a state of perpetual motion walking far and wide across the resort letting everyone know that it was her way or the highway. The exciting and vividly described stories of her past left no doubt that she was still very much with it. She was not a single pound overweight and although careful where she put her feet she kept moving ever onward. There is hope that no matter where you are from you can positively impact your state of health by making the effort.

A reader of my blog put is well when she offered her advice encouraging those in retirement to *get and stay as fit as possible and to do and go before good health and stamina abandon you. Such a large percentage of health issues for all Americans are the result of bad personal choices.*

We should not downplay the significance of eating right and exercising to encourage a healthier you. If you want to live a truly excellent retired life it helps to be healthy in mind and body. That said, I don't think we need to rehash the various philosophies of health or review the multitude of programs that can help to get you where you want to go. It would be surprising if you did not already have your favorite program or training routine by this point.

What I believe can be helpful is to highlight some simple and universal keys that apply across all programs intended to make you healthier. This is not a prescription for perfect health but rather observations made after many years attempting to stay on the healthy path as much as possible.

I am one of those fortunate folks who actually enjoy exercise and working out. Over the years I have created my own routine that combines cardiovascular for the old ticker, stretching via a combination of Yoga and Pilates to work the core and promote flexibility, and weight lifting to keep the biceps flex-worthy for as long as I can. I make exercises part of my every day. If I do not do something in the way of exercise each day, I miss it. If I miss two days in a row I actually feel a little bit off and even slightly agitated. Fortunately I know the cause of my restlessness and the cure is as simple as getting active and working out.

No matter how good it is for us, not everyone looks forward as I do to sweating on the bike or lifting weights. With that in mind I want to share a few practices that have worked for me over the years and might help in your efforts to do the right thing and live a healthier lifestyle. Don't expect anything earth shattering but rather some common sense principles to consider as you pursue your own good health in retirement.

Find an exercise that you can tolerate and stick with it

I wish I had started preparing sooner, but it's really never too late to improve your life and prepare for a healthier and more robust future.

To achieve results – short term as well as long term – you need to stick with it, whatever routine or program or combination of routines or programs you ultimately decide upon. You want to perform your exercises regularly and consistently. Busting your butt for a few months and then giving it up will not do much more than bust your butt.

If you hate what you are doing it will be difficult to maintain it. You will find excuses and you will likely fail. Though it may not be possible to find an exercise you actually enjoy at the very least try to find something that you can tolerate. Having a partner can help you on those days when you would rather be doing anything other than exercise. The two of you can push each other and support your common goals.

Try to think long term as you investigate the many options available. Healthy exercise and lifestyle is the job of a lifetime with no time off for good behavior. Realize that whatever you decide upon will become a part of your world for the foreseeable future. With that in mind you may want to include a variety of exercises and practices in your routine. Variety can help to keep things fresh as well as work different parts of your body in different ways.

Fortunately your choices of what exercises to do are seemingly endless with new programs popping up all the time. Had you heard of Zumba a year ago? Cross fitness sounded like some kind of clothing line until its recent rise to popularity. Yoga in its numerous forms and styles has grown impressively in popularity offering different strokes for different folks with very age appropriate options. For some having a set of barbells and an exercise bike in the garage is all it takes. Any of these options can help improve your health situation as long as you stick with it.

I know it takes work but the key is to start as early as you can and exercise, eat right and if you develop health issues, be proactive about managing them. Whatever your health issues are, there are things you can do to improve the quality of your life. My husband and I are almost 60 and we are both in really good health but we drink green smoothies daily, walk every evening and recently took up Tai Chi. I think many seniors just think ill health is part of life and they accept it without trying to improve the situation. Or they pop a pill and call it good.

So do your best to find something you enjoy or at least do not hate doing. Find a workout buddy who will motivate you when necessary and you them. Plan to stick with it long term to match your long term longevity target. And get ready to get healthy to enjoy that retirement you have worked so hard to get to.

Short cuts don't work long term

Don't try to fool yourself - staying healthy is a lifetime commitment. There are no quick and easy shortcuts. Diets and the latest and greatest fads may help you quickly drop a few pounds. But once you get to that reduced weight how do you maintain it? One diet prescribes no carbs while another supposedly equally effective option may require you eat nothing but carbs. One diet allows no fat consumption while the other allows for all the fat you want from meat, cheese and butter. Do you want to continue long term on a diet which although it may trigger a quick weight loss often excludes some part of a healthy balanced diet?

Although I do not personally like the idea of diets that generate quick reductions, I understand that for some therein lay the attraction. For a short term fix I will concede that a diet may have some value. After years of living with extra pounds it can feel good to lose that excess weight. That being the case, how much better would it be to sustain the loss beyond just the next weeks and months? Wouldn't you prefer a lifestyle adjustment that keeps you lean and mean for the foreseeable future? When it comes to doing the right things to live a healthy life, you don't want to cheat yourself. Play the game by the rules, accept that you will need to be living healthy for the rest of your days, and you are off to a good start.

Don't take the easy way take the exercise way
How many of us choose to take the elevator rather than walk a few flights to our destination? Or how often do we jump into the car to drive the few blocks to the local store? An easy way to add some exercise to your day is to choose to burn calories rather than store them. Use your legs rather than your rear end. Walk to the post office rather than drive. Get off your couch during halftime and move around. Don't look for the easy way to do things. Try to get yourself into the mindset of moving more. If you are sitting back and enjoying a long movie why not pick up some dumbbells and do a little lifting? Or stretch out on the floor and do some sit-ups? You can always do some stretching for flexibility even while continuing to watch your show. Be creative and be healthy

with a bit more movement and activity in your life. Don't look for the easy way, look for the exercise way.

I can't say how I'll feel in 25 years if I'm still around but I just hope I'm still out there going for my walks and doing Yoga. I've seen so many seniors just kind of give up and vegetate in old age. They won't eat right or go for walks or other simple things that would improve the quality of their life. What's the point of living to be old if you spend 15-20 years sitting and staring at the TV?

Everything in moderation
Temptations surround us. We each have our own special weaknesses whether wine or chocolate, cake or hamburgers, ice cream or chips. If we cannot control ourselves when it comes to these delicacies we can be in trouble. Man does not live by *(your favorite temptation here)* alone. However, in moderation with a modicum of control, giving into temptations can be acceptable. Too much of almost anything can be a bad thing.

Don't overdo it but on occasion it is okay to do it.

Watch what you eat
There are things out there that we simply should not put into our bodies. Some we may overlook unless we are vigilant such as preservatives, nitrites, sulfites, and various other –ites that do not add any nutritional value. Others we know darn well we should avoid or consciously minimize such

as fat, sugar, salt, and cholesterol. I have to confess that I have become an obsessive label reader. If it comes in a box or a bin or bottle or bag, I will look at the contents before buying it.

I need to watch my intake of various things to be good to my heart so my typical shopping spree goes something like this as I evaluate the worthiness of the foods I buy (note I am not a doctor – I just want to share how my mind works as I wander the isles at the local Safeway):

How much fat? I aim to keep my total consumption under 60 grams per day.

How much sodium? I target less than 1500 mcg per day maximum. This is tough if I even consider canned foods in the mix as they can exceed my daily allowance in a single serving.

Is there any cholesterol? The accepted dietary allowance is 300 mcg but I personally prefer to go for zero.

Are there preservatives? The more multiple syllable words on the label that I do not recognize the less likely I am to buy. I want to avoid nitrites as well which is painful as I love sausages and hotdogs both typically loaded with this evil. But I have found some chicken sausages that are spicy and very tasty with far less fat plus nitrite free to boot. If you are willing to take the time and test some options you can often find replacements for your favorite foods that are not so bad for you.

Is it natural? When it comes to meat I look for no antibiotics natural fed when possible and I am willing to pay the premium charged for a better knowledge of what I am eating.

For me label reading is second nature. It takes a few seconds and allows me to better manage what I put into my body. Once you find those offerings that are healthiest and tastiest you can stick with them and avoid the rest.

Take a nap
Often times there is nothing more refreshing than a quick 20 minute power nap. If you can close your eyes and shut off the world around you for just this brief amount of time you might be amazed how you feel when you awake. This skill is something I believe I inherited from my dad who used to come home from work at lunch and after eating a sandwich stretch out in the recliner for some quick shut eye. Within minutes he was asleep and when 20 minutes rolled around, he would awake and head back to work. After a power nap I feel myself ready to take on the world renewed. Now if there was just some way to incorporate naptime into our busy work day both employer and employee would likely benefit.

Do something with your spouse
My wife and I enjoy getting outside to hike the nearby hills or walk along the waterways or just wander our own neighborhood. We proceed at a brisk pace with a goal to cover at least five miles with me more often than not straining to keep up with her speedy gait. It is a perfect time to catch

up on each other's life while burning some calories to boot. Some complain that walking is not real exercise and that you need to get your heart rate higher to have any real value. But I figure that moving is better than sitting. And we love to explore nature around us under the warm sun so we plan to keep at it as long as we are able.

Other couples exercise and play together with a variety of activities from tennis to golf to kayaking to swimming. It is nice to do something together that you both enjoy and at the same time burn some calories.

You can't be good all the time
I am a firm believer in delayed gratification. In other words once you pay your dues you earn the right to be a little bit bad. I will religiously do my workouts each day – paying my dues. At the end of the day I will treat myself to a glass or two of wine – delayed gratification. My sister prefers her gratification in the form of chocolate – to each his or her own. But before you reap the rewards of your efforts you must expend the effort.

I think it is valuable to reward yourself on occasion. It is as important to live life and experience the pleasures and tastes and experiences it has to offer. Sacrifice and control are good to a point but don't be so strict that you allow yourself to miss out. A chocolate truffle so light yet rich that it makes your mouth water, that perfect cheesecake slice with just the right amount of tartness and creaminess, that decadent wurst with all the fixings – some of the simple pleasures of living. Not a part of our everyday diet but perhaps on occasion we can be a little bit bad. Just remember you will be paying your dues when it is all said and done and enjoy

Chapter 8 - Staying Busy and Engaged in Retirement

Men do not quit playing because they grow old;
they grow old because they quit playing.
~ Oliver Wendell Holmes

I want to retire! There is no doubt in my mind. The exact date is yet to be determined but there will definitely be a point in my life when I will leave my career aspirations behind and begin to live my second act. I can honestly say that I have enjoyed much of what I have done over these years on the job. I have met some wonderful people and achieved some worthy goals. I have had the opportunity to work in many different technologies under many different management styles. I can make a spreadsheet sing and throw out buzz words with the best of them. Yes, I can say that overall my work experiences have been relatively positive.

However, as with any job there have been moments that I would gladly have done without. I have been forced to deal with goals and quotas set unrealistically high, undermining the best efforts of my hard working sales reps. I have had to abruptly change direction with the introduction of new management and their ideas of how to run a successful company. I have been on the hot seat on occasion relentlessly grilled by unhappy executives explaining why the numbers were not achieved. And more than once I have had to deal with the purchase of my company by another entity that foists a big company mentality onto what had been a successful and exciting small company environment. I guess in the end a successful career really amounts to taking the good with the bad and ideally ending up with something worthwhile when everything is said and done.

I finished working some years ago, although I have only just reached official retirement age, and for some time I did find the transition from full time work to lady of leisure more problematic than I had expected. I guess I hadn't really factored in what I would be "losing" in addition to a monthly salary. Creating a sense of purpose to replace the imposed sense of purpose that work gives is something that I have long felt is a key to a happy retirement.

But someday I will be ready to retire. I imagine my day without the specter of work hovering and it makes me smile. I can already envision a typical day. First thing I will get up when I am ready to do so, not too early and not too late. I am not one to typically sleep in as I don't want to waste my day but one of the joys of being retired is it will be my choice to make. A nice cup of freshly brewed java and a casual reading of the newspaper are next on my "schedule". Then onward to the computer for an update from friends and family and a few hours spent writing my next work. When my creativity begins to dry up I will head to the local gym for my daily workout and then indulge myself in a nice lunch. Of course all of this happens at a pace that best suits my personal preference for that given day. I hope to live my retired life as I see fit in control at the helm steering in whatever direction most intrigues me for the moment.

Not a bad plan if I may say so myself. And I truly believe that I can handily keep myself occupied for the first half of my day. But then things can start to get a bit iffy. Assuming I am done with lunch at 1:00, I will still have five hours until dinner. And then after dinner some additional hours remain to be filled before bedtime. And then it all starts over again tomorrow.

One of my biggest fears in living a fulfilling retirement is not having enough meaningful activities and pursuits to fill my days. Yes I have hobbies and sure my to-do list typically includes a handful of things just waiting to be done. But is there enough to last an entire year? What about 10 years? What about 20 years? If we retire at age 65 we can hope for another 20 plus years of retirement. How the heck will I stay busy with worthwhile activities for such an extended period?

More is not necessarily better

I am one of those enjoyers that does less and at my own pace. While I understand that some people need to feel busy all the time in retirement and continually challenged, I think most retirees enjoy their ability to go half pace. Some retirees will be active. Some will move to an extremely slow lifestyle and be fulfilled over the long run. I personally prefer the extremely slow lifestyle with some travel and activity thrown in here and there.

At the crux of my dilemma is the nature of what I will do when I am retired. For me living an active life is not just about keeping busy. It is about engaging in activities that are meaningful and worthwhile. It is about doing something that matters. It is about arriving at the end of the day to look back on what I did and experiencing a feeling of accomplishment. I did not just kill off the hours but made them count.

That said, I am not suggesting that every little thing I will do must have some redeeming value. Nor am I saying that I feel the need to do something to fill every available moment in the day. A rewarding life is not just about seeing more, doing more, tasting more and experiencing more. It is about maintaining a balance between doing and not doing, engaging and relaxing, gearing up and shutting down. We have a better chance of enriching our being if we try to focus on the quality of our experiences not obsess about the quantity. Imagine someone wandering through the mighty Louvre. What a terrible mistake to try to see everything you possibly can with your limited time. You are doomed before taking your first step. By trying to see everything you more likely end up retaining little and finding yourself exhausted. It would be better to sit in front of that one painting you really enjoy and take it in, appreciate it, see it from all perspectives and walk away with an indelible memory of one positive experience. How much more enjoyable to give yourself a chance to absorb and process the experience rather than bombard yourself with sensory overload.

While planning and preparing for a happy retirement life, it can be helpful to dig into exactly what it is that we will do to occupy our days. Try not to think in terms of just keeping busy but instead what will we do to add real meaning and worth to our day. In my book *"Are You Just Existing and Calling it a Life?"* I discuss the importance of taking time to search for and discover your individual passion. What is it that drives you, inspires you, and empowers you and can ultimately give meaning and purpose to your life beyond merely existing? What specifically is it that you love to do and would continue loving to do years from now? Is there something in your life that when discussed with others can trigger excitement in you to the extent that you can hardly shut up? If you have not yet found this imagine discovering such a passion before you begin your retired life and then pursuing it in retirement!

Do not accept a role of merely existing. Don't spend all of your retirement sitting safely on the sidelines passively watching the world go by. Retirement can be a time to try those things you have always wanted but were prevented by life circumstances. It can be an awakening of the inner you who has been stymied within an uninspired job. It can be your chance to step outside of the box that has defined you and try new things.

Find a happy medium between activity and relaxation

None of us wants to be bored in our retirement. We hope to identify projects and passions and hobbies and travels that will keep us busy and engaged so we live a meaningful life. But it is not just about keeping busy. Retirement is also our time to slow down and relax. Without the burden of a working life or the responsibility of raising our family, we actually have the time to do nothing. We have the opportunity to sleep in, savor a peaceful morning, enjoy a casual walk, and basically live our life at a pace that is perfect for us. It is helpful to factor in the natural slowing down that is part of our aging.

Once retired, we will assume responsibility for maintaining a balance between activity and relaxation. A retired life made up of only one or the other does not typically work well. Both are important ingredients. And one of the joys of this time in our life is we are in control of what and where we wish to focus our attention. A mix of activity then some down time, an adventure then a vacation, a physically taxing outing and then a quiet nap in the garden. We get to find that right combination that matches our individual tastes. It is all about achieving balance.

Balance, to me, is the key. Being on the go is fine in my opinion, but to be able to do it with less stress is what retirement is all about. Retirement is not an either-or phenomenon. It is not slow suicide or another version of the rat-race. I work hard at: golf, banjo, grand parenting, reading, puppeteering, etc. They used to be ways to get away from the stressful gerbil cage of work. Now they are opportunities to hone my mind and soul. They are sources of social networking and sharing. I am still in the world at large.

Don't limit yourself to "what you should be doing"

Have you ever found yourself excited about a new adventure you are about to undertake and wanting to share with a family member or close friend? And when you tell them the response is like a wet towel thrown on your dreams as they suck the joy right out of your moment. *Are you sure you want to do that? Is that what people your age are doing these days? I don't know, that sounds pretty risky.* If you too easily take their thoughtless words to heart, you can find yourself doubting your earlier conviction. What was such a clear and inspired plan mere moments ago may suddenly sound like a pipe dream with little likelihood of being realized. Now you know what a train feels like when it is derailed.

Retirement is not the time to only do what you are supposed to be doing. Retirement is your time to do what you want to be doing. You know that stack of books patiently waiting on the shelves, books that you have no interest in reading but somehow ended up in your possession over the years? There is nothing that says you have to read them. How about picking out those that look good and donating the rest to the community library?

Climb Machu Picchu at age 60 – are you out of your mind? If you feel that this is something you really want to do and if you are physically and financially able to pursue it, why not go for it? If this is your chance to pursue a dream you have always had, try not to let yourself be swayed by advice from naysayers who lack the courage to pursue their own passions.

We are getting ready for our third big retirement trip - one month in Rome while we recover from one month in energetic Buenos Aires. Originally, I kept thinking, "Are we too old to travel?" Glad I ignored my doubts.

Learn to dance the tango, try your hand at snowboarding, parasailing can be quite a rush I hear, create a comic strip, get involved with local politics, start your own website or blog, build a gazebo in your backyard, learn to scuba, take advantage of your freedom to spend your time doing what it is that you really want to do despite the protestations of those less adventurous.

When it comes to what we choose to do with our retired life it would be a mistake to limit our options based upon guidelines and rules that apply to others. We are responsible for creating that fulfilling retired life that works best for our situation.

Doing what is appropriate for your age is up to you to define. What others may roll their eyes at might be exactly right for you. You can set your own rules, follow your own dreams, ignore what others may say, and do it. What you should be doing is what you want to be doing!

What's your talent?
My wife and I were recently at a gathering of local musicians and lovers of good food, people who had come together to share snacks and wine and listen to songs presented by a few of the attendees. Everyone was excited, friendly, and looking forward to sitting down to some good tunes. While we were mingling, one of the musicians asked my wife, "What's your talent?" I had never thought in those terms before but what an excellent question. Later in the evening while doing his musical set, he even mentioned a study he had read that said we only use 25 percent of our talent on a regular basis.

For most of the attendees that evening, music and art was a common theme. We had a mix of singers and performers, a handful of artists including a French sculptor, and a few of us who were there to listen to the musical talent. But what was my talent? What was it that I was personally good at? Yes I had my share of piano lessons as a kid and could jingle the keyboards a bit. I was also getting into writing between my blogs and books. I realized that I had a certain flair for putting together a nice arrangement of plants in the garden. But I have to say that question really got me thinking and I find the answers are still evolving.

By the way, what's your talent?

Try something new

The best thing about retirement is that one can go in many directions to pursue those hobbies and likes that work got in the way of pursuing. Among the many passions that I have had is the opportunity to explore the hobby of ballroom dancing, traveling the world as a Cruise Ship Dance Host and seeing most of the warm ports of the world. Also, by retiring from teaching I now have the opportunity to still be in the classroom when I want to be and when I have the time to be as a substitute teacher. There is nothing like having a career you can modify and pursue when you choose to.

So you need some help identifying possible interests to pursue once you retire? Here is a collection of 77 suggestions (don't ask me why that particular number). Realize this is only a partial list of the limitless options you have available to explore. Consider it a starting point, presented for you to peruse, consider, ignore, or check into as you see fit:

- Break out the old fishing pole
- Think of activities you have loved to do in the past and give them another try
- Take a class in drawing
- Learn a new language
- Become a substitute teacher
- Try your hand at photography – you will be surprised what your smart phone is capable of
- Take up a musical instrument
- Write a story or a book
- Explore Ikebana
- Form a band
- Travel to locations with historical significance for your own family and ancestors
- Plant a flower garden
- Write a song
- Take an online course in whatever strikes your fancy
- Ride a horse
- Write a poem
- Visit a local library, home to a multitude of books, videos and more
- Take a class in drawing or sculpting or other art expressions
- Pick up a jigsaw puzzle – especially fun if your spouse also has the bug
- Plant a vegetable garden
- Learn to play bridge
- Learn to play chess or learn to play it better

- Try Sudoku – way beyond me but my wife is a pro
- Take a trip near or far
- Learn to cook
- Get yourself in better physical shape
- Take a cruise
- Try bird watching
- Try your hand at landscaping
- Start a business
- Take up golf
- Become a blogger
- Add a pet to the family
- Take up hiking
- Make your own clothes
- Volunteer
- Go fly a kite
- Learn Photoshop and become a face swapper
- Catch up on your movies
- Catch up on your books
- Try meditation
- Help out at a local school or church
- Try Yoga
- Join a club
- Start a club – online communities are easy and very interactive
- Make your own greeting cards – very personal, very witty
- Document your family history in pictures and stories
- Create a family tree
- Set up a Facebook account and see what it is all about
- See if wine tasting is to your liking

- Paint or decorate a room
- House swap for a new perspective
- Dust off the old bike and ride the neighborhoods
- Become a tutor or mentor
- Learn to throw darts
- Try hot air ballooning
- Go back to school for a degree in something you love
- Visit all of the California missions
- Set up your own website
- Ride a motorcycle
- Revisit a hobby from your youth
- Check out an RV and hit the road
- Follow your favorite sports team to games
- Track down earlier classmates to re-establish contact
- Tramp through Europe
- Look into a part time job
- Become an expert – it takes 10,000 hours
- Make humorous personalized tee shirts or mugs or mouse pads
- Try your hand at remote control helicopters, cars, boats and even animals
- Visit a museum
- Make a video
- Go to the park or zoo
- Go snorkeling
- Meet your neighbors
- Take a dance lesson
- Try selling your artistic creations at local art fairs or flea markets
- Check into coin or stamp collecting
- Become a star gazer

Feel free to step outside your comfort zone, take a chance, and explore the many available options. In reality the list of possibilities is endless.

Chapter 9 - What Retirement is Not

Life is a series of natural and spontaneous changes. Don't resist them – that only creates sorrow. Let reality be reality. Let things flow naturally forward in whatever way they like.
~ Lao Tzu

Retirement will be many things to many people. It offers a chance to create a made-just-for-you life that evolves over years of living it. As you proceed you can try different things, fine tune where needed, make some mistakes along the way and ultimately if successful, create the retirement package ideal for you. It is a journey rather than a destination. In the beginning it can be difficult to have a clear view of what lies ahead. But a central theme remains that this is your time to do what you want to do, to do it when you want, and to do it for as long as you want.

Technically retirement begins when you decide it is time to exit your job. Initially it may be the escape from the pressures and stress of our work career that we find most attractive about retiring. Whether you enjoyed your job or despised it, a time will come when you are done, you have had enough, fine, nada mas. It is time to turn the page to the next chapter to see what more life has to offer. Unfettered by work's responsibilities we envision days spent in pursuit of passions and promise, experimenting with new things, traveling to our hearts content, or doing whatever it may be that strikes our fancy. The real beauty is our ability to choose what we will do. After years of putting our wishes and dreams on hold to meet the responsibilities of job and family, this new found freedom can be a breath of fresh air. Retirement may be the first time in our life when we have the chance to step out and cut loose and explore the real person we are inside.

As we look ahead and plan for an exciting and fulfilling retirement, it can be helpful to realize that there are some things retirement is not. After all of our reading and research, despite our diligent planning and preparation, our picture of retirement may still be somewhat distorted.

Our not-so-Golden Years

I go along with the general consensus that once we leave work behind and are able to do more of what we actually want to do, we are entering a wonderful time in our lives. But I do not necessarily agree with the Golden Years moniker. There are too many factors that can quickly tarnish any 24 carat shine on our retirement years. The reality is that unless we retire early, we are talking about starting this new chapter at 65 or older. Yes people are living longer and the continuing medical advances have been nothing short of phenomenal. But no one can indefinitely escape the inevitability of time and the toll it takes on us physically and often mentally as we progress into those later years.

Get ready to start moving a bit more slowly, seeing a bit less clearly, forgetting a bit more frequently, and straining to hear the world around you. Should you advance well into those Golden Years you can expect to gradually sacrifice your independence as you are no longer able to safely care for all your needs. Prepare for others to start making decisions that impact you directly. And though intended to be in your best interest, you may not always see it as such. Say goodbye to your keys should the time come that you cannot safely negotiate the highways and byways. That freedom to take control of what we do can be replaced with the harsh reality that we are losing that very independence that made retirement so attractive at the outset.

Retirement may not be entirely the best years of our lives but they should also not be the worst. Our best equipment to mitigate the challenges of age may come down to maintaining as positive an attitude and outlook as we can. Reality is what it is and we cannot skirt the issues. We can choose to obsess and focus on the negatives and succumb without a fight. Or we can do our best to focus on the positive, any positive, to improve the quality of our life. See the cup as half full, appreciate the beauty of a sunrise and sunset, share in the joy witnessed in the smile on the face of a child, hang on a bit longer to that loving hug, smile in the face of adversity, try to do those little things with a positive outlook and thankfulness that we are alive to experience the moment. Anyway, that is the route I hope to take.

I retired two years ago and found myself in a state of desperation and confusion. I did not have a clue and did not prepare or plan for the non-financial component of the retirement process – my grave mistake and I greatly suffered for it. Slowly, patiently, I found my path to a comfortable and meaningful retirement through reading books, articles from the Internet, magazines, and newspapers. It reminds me of a quote from Robert Frost, "In three words I can sum up everything I've learned about life – it goes on."

So it is true that much of our retirement can be just what we imagine as we explore and try new things free from the distractions that filled our life with such details as keeping our job and getting the kids through college. No argument there. However I still have a problem with its Golden depiction of all things wonderful. We will have challenges, not all will be easy, we may find ourselves bored, we will find ourselves slowing down but hopefully we can experience more good than bad. With that in mind I might propose we reclassify our retirement as those magical **Silver Years** of living. Not quite golden in quality but better than bronze. And nicely synchronized with the color of the hair on our retired heads!

A safe haven

So you have made the move into retirement and are spreading your wings as a new retiree. It feels good to put the stressful working world behind and you are optimistic about what this new chapter might hold. Now all you have to do is figure out how to keep yourself busy and go about pursuing all those passions you are anxious to immerse yourself in. The hard part is over and now its smooth sailing ahead, right? Not so fast.

Here are the two major reasons that Americans and Canadians have money problems regardless of how much they make:
(1) Delayed gratification takes too long;
(2) A necessity is any luxury that the neighbor happens to have.

Unless you are independently wealthy, you will probably never be free of nagging concerns over your finances. You may believe you have saved a sufficient amount to allow you to withdraw a reasonable percentage over your years in retirement to live a good life. Your financial planner hopefully has your investments diversified to spread out your risk. You have calculated the right age to start receiving your Social Security benefits so as to insure yourself against extreme old age. What is there to worry about? Don't look now but consider a few disheartening possibilities: the next recession or depression gets under way; a war breaks out somewhere and causes worldwide concern; the next bubble runs its course and bursts impacting everyone in its wake; a new financial program is created that no one really understands, everyone gets into, and eventually proves to be nothing more than smoke and mirrors; Congress stalls making important decisions for too long and we all lose; things get tough for your kids and they are forced to move in with you, family and all; the list goes on. The bottom line is that you can do everything in your power to provide for your financial well being in retirement. But there are events beyond your control that can nonetheless impact you directly. Worrying will not prevent it from happening but sometimes even that is beyond our control.

Consider also that your health at the date of your retirement will likely be the best it is ever going to be. Of course you can start living healthier and exercising more and eating well in which case you might improve your situation to some degree. But the fact is you are getting older and that wonderful body that has carried you faithfully to this point in time is going to start falling a bit short of what you wish were its capabilities. It doesn't get any easier but at least if you are on a gradual decline you have a chance to adapt. It can be worse if your health suddenly gives out and you find yourself on a quick decline. In such a case your carefully laid retirement plans will have to be adjusted as best you are able. Just when you thought you safely arrived, you may find yourself forced to deal with a host of new and unpredictable challenges.

A time to just watch life from the sidelines

Exactly what is retirement? Sitting around with nothing left to do? Not on your life! The most boring useless retirement to me is spent golfing, eating out and constantly travelling – all just to stay busy. Living in South Florida, I saw this repeated over and over. Also, a 'retirement community' for perfectly healthy people is a trap. Get out of your age group! Stop obsessing on your multi-aches and pains (I realize some folks have more than others), going to the doctor should not be your big day out. See your whole community as it is. Volunteer where your heart calls you. Nothing is life is more important than people.

We have all seen the travel advertisement or media depiction of the happy retired couple sitting peacefully together watching the world go by. If their faces are visible there will surely be a happy if not slightly mindless smile splashed broadly across their countenance. They may be sitting on a bench watching the waves or sitting on a park bench watching the squirrels or sitting on rockers on a peaceful deck overlooking a lake. The common thread here is they are sitting. And they are doing nothing. If you were to believe the scene as an accurate depiction, retirement is really nothing more than moving your seat from in front of the TV to a different location where you can continue your couch potato ways. Is that really what it is all about?

Retirement does not have to be a time for merely observing life from the sidelines. Living your retired life to its fullest does not have to be about accepting a role of merely existing where you live safely on the periphery passively watching the world go by. Friedrich Nietzsche said *"Is not life a hundred times too short for us to bore ourselves?"* Your retirement can be your chance to step outside of the box that has defined who you are and start to explore those things that will define who you want to be. Now you have the time to follow those passions that were stifled in your role as a loyal worker bee. You can make that bucket list of things you have always wanted to do and start doing them. Don't wait for something to happen, make something happen.

Think back to a time when you were hard at work diligently pursuing your job. Outside the day was bright and sunny with life busting out all over in the blooming trees and singing birds. And maybe you caught a glimpse of a youngster traipsing through the leaves or chasing a ball or just twirling in joy at their freedom from responsibility and worry. If you did not feel a bit of envy at that moment you would not be human. Retirement can be your chance to experience like that child freedom from responsibility and care. Will you choose to sit on a bench and calmly watch the world go by? Or will you step up and live your retirement to the fullest? Your retirement does not have to be a place to hide from the world. Rather it can be a new launch point from which you will journey into adventures and experiences worthy of that creative passionate person you are.

Dazed and confused about retirement and aging is putting it mildly. At issue is how to find some peace with myself which at times seems unreachable. I've read all the stuff on so called encore careers but for me somehow all that seems like a brass ring on the carousel that I can't seem to emotionally or mentally reach. Some of this is combined with the not so pleasant realities of aging. The bottom line is that I can't seem to shake this new reality and find a regenerative way "out" that makes sense.

Chapter 10 – Staying Safe in Retirement

*Who can hope to be safe? Who sufficiently
cautious?*
*Guard himself as he may, every moment is an
ambush. ~ Horace*

The older we get the more we tend to appreciate
life for all it is and has to offer. Those little things
we took for granted while young can now hold
much more significance. We begin to contemplate
our own mortality and if smart we are thankful for
each day with which we are blessed. We also
begin to realize that we might not be as invincible
at 65 as we were at 25. A tumble while we were
young was something to laugh about while at a
more advanced age can have serious long term
ramifications. And so we may become a bit more
cautious in our endeavors, a bit more aware of
risky situations and ever conscious of our
vulnerabilities.

No none wants to live their retirement in undue
fear. This is our time to enjoy the life we have
been forced to delay while we paid our dues and
survived the perils of parenthood. Now is the time
to experiment and explore, to travel and try new
things, to venture out into this magnificent world
around us. Living each day entails a certain
amount of risk taking. Just crossing the street can
be dangerous and driving in high speed freeway
traffic where not everyone is paying close attention

can be chilling. Sharp knives, running with scissors, slipping on a wet surface, getting chased by a stray dog, lightening strikes, climbing a ladder to change a bulb, the list goes on and on.

In the end we will agree to accept some degree of risk in many of our endeavors. But as we age it can become more important to weigh the costs and benefits of taking those risks. There is nothing wrong with a little safety first perspective. As a retiree to be, we can incorporate our new found respect for safety into the retirement environment we want to experience.

Stay safe around the home
Many retirees hope to retire in the home in which they currently reside. Familiar surroundings within a well known neighborhood eating at restaurants long ago identified as favorite is their idea of the perfect retirement life. Why think of moving elsewhere when things are perfect where you are? And as long as you maintain good health and can afford to do so, it is a win-win situation.

But as we begin to venture into our later years that home sweet home environment may become a bit less friendly and in some situations even dangerous. Too many steps to get to the bedroom, poor lighting that hides sharp edges, bathrooms with slippery floors, all these can prove hazardous to the aged resident. Easy to cope with when we are younger, they can prove dangerous to brittle bones and less than perfect eyesight.

If we wish to remain in place during our retirement years we can take steps to prepare our home environment to fit our changing needs. There is a concept called Universal Design that came about after World War II to address the needs of returning veterans and the disabled. Wikipedia defines this as *broad-spectrum architectural planning ideas meant to produce buildings, products and environments that are inherently accessible to both the able-bodied and the physically disabled.* Today, this concept has been expanded to address the requirements of senior living. Properly implemented, universal design can make a big difference in facilitating independent retirement living.

Bathrooms can be one of the most dangerous rooms in the house. How many of us know of someone who has fallen in the bathroom and done them self serious harm? We know how important it is to take steps to prevent slipping in the tub or shower. Non-slip strips and floors on showers and tubs is a must with support bars offering an added safety measure. Bath tubs can now be had with doors to enter instead of having to climb down into the tub. Showers that are flush to the floor, with no edge to step over are another good idea. Toilets that are at a comfortable height will be well appreciated. Faucets that are easily turned on and off and adjusted to the right temperature can help to prevent burns.

An effectively laid out **kitchen** can increase the user friendliness for senior inhabitants. AARP indicates that the kitchen is the single place where universal design can have the most impact. Counter tops should be at an easily accessible height. Side by side refrigerators are easier to negotiate than those with freezers either above or below. Storage should allow easy access to contents via pull out drawers or lazy-Susan-type devices. Faucets are easiest to control with a single lever instead of multiple knobs for hot and cold. Something as simple as a non-slip rug in front of the sink can make the kitchen area a bit safer.

Good **lighting** throughout the house is important as well. I know we try to save energy and I am all for it but the fact is: stronger bulbs shed more light. Make sure to illuminate any potentially hazardous areas such as steps leading into the house or unexpected obstacles in the home or yard. Motion detecting fixtures can be helpful as they activate when entering an area without the need to manually turn them on. Light switches are available with a large flat panel area instead of the old flip switch, easier to quickly turn on without having to blindly fumble for that tiny switch. And you can get lamps that are activated by a simple touch rather than switch – pretty cool. Do you remember the advertisement for the Clapper – "Clap on, clap off, the Clapper." This simple plug you insert in the socket and then plug in your lamp allows you to clap your hands to turn on and off the attached light.

I recommend handles rather than knobs for interior doors. Not only do they allow you to open a door with just one hand but they are easier to manage especially with arthritis or decreased strength. Make sure that cabinet knobs and handles are big enough to easily grasp.

Around the home, attention to the little things can help make a safer more retiree-friendly environment in which to enjoy your days.

Act defensively
My dad warned me many years ago that the most dangerous place to drive is a parking lot. People find themselves in close quarters with other cars driven by distracted drivers of all ages and levels of experience or as is often the case inexperience. Some look behind before they back out others just roll the dice and back on out. Pedestrians meander around with their thoughts far away or attention riveted to their iPhone waiting pensively for that oh so important next Facebook update. In general it is safe to assume no one is paying attention as they should to what they are doing. It is a perfect storm inviting accidents of all kinds.

Dad always said you need to assume that those around you are going to make a mistake, do the wrong thing or in some way just blow it. See that car maneuvering to pull out in front of you? You are well advised to assume they are going to cut you off or worse yet hit you. If you take on a defensive posture you can be better prepared to quickly react and get out of harm's way. Expect the worst and be pleasantly surprised when things turn out okay.

This kind of thinking can fit nicely into everyday life of senior citizens as they navigate the world around them. For example, when you are crossing the street in the crosswalks with the walk signal flashing, don't assume that the car approaching the intersection sees you. Wait until they slow to a stop before venturing in harm's way. I like to look the driver directly in the eyes until making contact so I know they do in fact see me. When you receive an unsolicited email from someone you think you know, be careful about clicking on any links. I am sure you would rather miss seeing a cute picture of a cat chasing its shadow than launch a virus in your computer. When you enter your password at the ATM use your body to block the view from those in line. If the road ahead looks slippery assume it is and be doubly cautious. Try to do those little things that can make you safer going through your daily routines.

Try to maintain a general watchfulness in all of your activities so you become a less inviting target. Walk well-lighted streets at night and remain aware of your surroundings. Do your shopping with someone else rather than alone.

You do not want to become an overly-paranoid retiree but neither do you want to leave yourself needlessly open to harm nor exploitation. Do your best to pay attention and keep your eyes open, ever watchful and aware of your surroundings.

Don't do it all yourself

It can be difficult to accept we are no longer that young spring chicken we were some years ago. The reality is some things that we took for granted might start to be too much for us to safely handle. The sooner we realize and come to terms with this the better we will be. The consequences of attempting to do more than we are capable of doing can be disastrous with broken limbs, bumped heads, and bruised pride the potential outcome. Rather than risk injury, why not reach out to someone younger with better balance and much superior recuperative powers?

Personally I have a fear of heights so it is not asking too much for me to seek assistance when it comes to anything involving a ladder or activity conducted from a height greater than ten feet. Cleaning the gutters of old leaves, putting up Christmas lights, pruning branches of tall trees in the backyard, anything involving being up on the roof of your house – these are all perfect opportunities to enlist the aid of a member from the younger generation. I have had an aversion to power saws ever since my pediatrician sliced of two fingers while cutting a board. He was pretty calm under fire as he scooped up the fingers, put them on ice in a plastic bag, and drove himself to the emergency room. I do not think I would have reacted quite so calmly or efficiently. Electricity is also something that I was never good at and so have no problem calling in reinforcements should a short happen or a fixture need replacement.

Another helpful piece of advice is to think twice before attempting to lift heavy things. In the old days I used to drag refrigerators up the steps and move heavy furniture with wild reckless abandon. These days I look to my son and his strong friends to do the deed. I know too many people who have attempted to lift something heavier than they should whose backs suffered as a result.

I have accepted that there are areas where I lack expertise as well as activities that may put me at risk of hurting myself. At age 40 I did not think twice and just gave it my best shot. However, as this retiree to be plans for his later years, I will have to learn on occasion to hand over the reins to those whose hips can heal quickly should an accident occur.

Of course we all have different comfort levels and different experience so I am not suggesting you give up those activities which you can still safely and effectively undertake. But it is within our power to reduce our exposure to possible harm by being cautious with some things. We all want to maintain our independence for as long as is humanly possible. But discretion can be the better part of valor and you cannot undo a broken hip.

Prepare for emergencies
Bad things can happen to good people despite our best precautions. Although we cannot prevent occasionally stumbling along the way we can prepare ourselves to better react when emergencies occur. A little preparation can go a long way to assist in dealing effectively with an emergency and may also provide a little peace of mind knowing you have a clearly defined course of action should it be needed.

One thing you should do today is create a list of all medications and dosages that you take and put it in your wallet. This is vital information for doctors and hospitals in case something unexpected happens to you and you are unable to communicate your information. It takes a few minutes and can be a big help should it be needed. Just write down the prescription name, dosage, and the frequency at which you take your pills.

We live in California and so are quite familiar with earthquakes. The 7.1 magnitude Loma Prieta quake of 1989 had its epicenter six miles from our home. Our chimney collapsed, the house was knocked off its foundation, the water heater ripped from its stand, and we were without water and electricity for more than two days. The earthquake itself created rolling waves in the asphalt, collapsed the Bay Bridge and resulted in serious fires in San Francisco. We know what can happen and that it can and will happen again.

To prepare for an earthquake you should set aside those necessary food, water, clothing, and supplies to sustain you in case the rest of the world comes to a standstill. The USGS has a very helpful 32 page book specific to California that talks about the nature and history of earthquakes in California as well as how to prepare and respond. Although specific to California it includes excellent pointers that are applicable no matter where you live. You can download your own copy of the book at
http://www.earthquakecountry.info/roots/PuttingDownRootsSoCal2011.pdf

A few quick additions from personal experience: First, have the phone number of a contact out of state that all family members can call in the event of an earthquake or other disaster. Phone lines in the affected area will be jammed with people frantically calling each other. If everyone checks in to the shared number you can avoid some anxious moments. Second, keep a supply of your medications accessible, enough for at least one week. Be sure to keep these up to date by rotating them every year. Lastly keep the propane tank filled for your gas barbeque. This turned out to be a huge help for us back during Loma Prieta. With no electricity the contents of our refrigerator and freezer were not going to survive. So we took out all the meat and had a big barbeque. A few friends found their way to our place and we sat in the backyard comforting one another as aftershocks rumbled every few minutes. We also had a few bottles of champagne in the refrigerator that we did not want to go to waste. Looking back I believe we made the best of a difficult situation!

Depending on where you live, you and your family will be exposed to other natural disasters ranging from floods to tornados, from seasonal fires to hurricanes. Take the time to prepare a plan with a defined course of action for the emergency situations most common to your location. Even if you never use them, the peace of mind in your preparedness will be well worth the time and effort.

Beware Scammers
I hold a generally optimistic outlook on life and have always believed we should have faith in others. People are as a whole good and worthy of being trusted. Yes, I have been proved wrong on occasion over the years, but I still prefer to maintain this point of view regarding the nature of the human species. Unfortunately it can be just this innocent view of the world that criminals seek to exploit when it comes to senior citizens.

One of my blog readers tells how spammers targeted him: *My wife and I were visiting with her cousin when my cell phone rang. I answered, "Hello", and a voice on the other end said, "For your security, please enter your social security number now." Naturally I simply hung up the phone. But I got to thinking about the scam and supposed that if this auto dialer were to call 10,000 or so phone numbers, I'd bet that a handful of unfortunate persons would enter their social security number.*

To prevent becoming another victim, it helps to be constantly on our guard and ever vigilant. Before you open your wallet or share personal information, be sure you are dealing with a legitimate concern. It is easier to avoid becoming a victim of a scam than try to fix something once you have been caught up in the scheme.

There are some common red flags to be on the watch for:
1. "You must act now" – scammers often pressure you to act immediately before you have time to think over their offer. Beware any "limited time only" or "you must act now" offers.
2. Promises of something free – offering a freebie to get you excited is an often used trick. Beware if you are then asked to pay shipping or processing in order to receive your free offer. Once they have your credit information it can be used for much more than a simple shipping charge.
3. Watch for misspellings or obvious grammatical errors in emails. Also pay attention for fraudulent calls that refer to an organization incorrectly. For example the American Diabetes Association

incorrectly referenced as the "Diabetic Association".

4. False claims of endorsement from well-known organizations – if the caller claims the organization has a good Better Business Bureau rating go to the BBB site and check them out.

5. Go with your gut – if the offer sounds fishy or too good to be true, walk away.

Here is a list of some of the more common scams being perpetrated on unsuspecting victims.

Relative in distress call - you receive a panicked call from someone identifying himself as a relative asking for money because he was just in an accident. You must act immediately or they will go to jail. If you agree you are either asked to wire the money or they will send a second party to your door to collect it. To prevent becoming a victim, confirm that the caller is your relative by asking questions that only he would know. Don't be tricked into acting before you fully understand what is going on. Don't take any action unless you are 100% sure and trust your gut.

Repair and contracting scams – in addition to honest hard working contractors there are criminals that take advantage of unsuspecting homeowners. When it comes to assuring legitimate home repairs, red flags to watch for include asking for a large amount of money up front, pressure to act now to take advantage of a limited time special offer, or a knock at the door from a contractor who just happened to be in the area (sometimes while you are talking a second person sneaks into your house to burglarize you). None of these are typical of how honest contractors work.

Before you agree to anything talk to references and examine the quality of work done. Get quotes in writing and seek multiple bids to compare. Ask friends for their recommendations. Ask the contractor for their license number. In California, the State License Board administers examinations to test prospective licensees, issues licenses, investigates complaints against licensed and unlicensed contractors, issues citations, suspends or revokes licenses, and seeks administrative, criminal, and civil sanctions against violators. Better safe than sorry. Check out the Better Business Bureau listings for accredited contractors. Do your research before investing what can be significant sums of money.

Check cashing and money order scams – someone you are doing business with 'accidently' sends you a check for more than the amount they owe you. They then ask you to deposit the check and wire them the difference. The money wired arrives immediately while the check clearing process may take a few days. Say goodbye to your money. If someone sends you the incorrect amount simply ask them to send a new check with the right dollars reflected. You can tear up or send back their erroneous check.

Identify theft – once your identity has been stolen your bank accounts, credit cards and credit rating are in serious jeopardy. Scams run the gamut from grandchildren stranded in foreign countries to unknown charities asking for your contributions to credit card companies supposedly updating your information. Legitimate companies will not ask for personal information via email. Never give your personal financial information to unsolicited callers. If something appears fishy don't take a chance.

If you believe your identify may have been stolen, contact your credit and debit card companies and request new cards. Report the incident to the Federal Trade Commission at their website www.ftc.gov/idtheft.This will allow the FTC to identify patterns associated with the unauthorized transactions and investigate the source of the data breach. Again it is far better to err on the side of caution up front. Once your identity is stolen you can be in for a long and painful road trying to correct the crime.

Jury duty scam - a caller claims to be a jury coordinator. If you explain that you never received a summons for jury duty, the scammer asks you for your Social Security number and date of birth so he can verify the information and cancel the arrest warrant that will otherwise be issued. Should you give out this information your identity can be stolen. Instead make a call to city hall and find out for yourself from a legitimate employee.

Telemarketing fraud – anytime you hear "free" and "must act now" in the same discussion beware. High pressure phone sales people are trained to say just the right thing and apply pressure to get you to act now before you have a chance to research what you are getting into. If the caller is not willing to give you time to check them out and push for immediate action they could have something to hide.

Phishing scams – you receive an email supposedly from a legitimate financial institution asking you to update your account information. You click on a link and end up at a fake banking site that steals your information. Some creative crooks have even used the Better Business Bureau scam where the subject line is "complaint against your business". By clicking on the attachment or link you download malware that discovers your personal financial information. Legitimate businesses will not ask for personal information or passwords via email – it is just not safe.

Lottery scams – who among us has not received an email saying we have won thousands or even millions of dollars in some lottery that we have never participated in nor likely even heard of. Supposedly you have won tons of money – you just need to send a small amount to handle the administrative costs. Since no legitimate lottery asks for fees or notifies you by email, do not get suckered into this scheme.

You've got the job scam – for anyone looking for work the promise of a job can be tempting. You receive an email that directs you to what looks like a legitimate website. You have a phone interview and then hear the good news that the job is yours! All you have to do is complete a credit report with all of your personal financial information. Run away.

I think the best strategy is to follow the old adage "trust but verify". We can give someone the benefit of the doubt initially but before we take action or share our personal information we confirm the legitimacy of the offer. Yes I believe you but just let me double check.

Drive a senior safe car
Driving safely is challenging at any age with traffic, constant road repairs, unexpected detours, and bad weather conditions. For older drivers the effects of aging on reaction time and vision can make things even more difficult. According to AAA in Washington, D.C., 90 percent of drivers age 65 or older experience health issues ranging from arthritis to diminished vision that can impact their safe driving efforts. Since many of us will drive into our eighties why not look for those features and capabilities in a car that enable us to more safely navigate the roads? Let's start with seats that

allow for multi-position adjustments and fine tuning to our particular posture and comfort. Sexy sport seats may look good but can be uncomfortable for any extended period of driving. A nice feature to include is the heated seat for those cold mornings. When you get into in a cold car to start your day a little warmth from beneath can go a long way to thaw you out.

If your eyesight is not what it used to be look for big, well illuminated dials and controls on the dashboard. Digital readouts are easy to spot and make it more obvious how fast you are going in a quick glance. You will also benefit from large windows that offer clear line of sight. The small sexy windows typical of sport cars and rocket ships can easily present blind spots and make it difficult to see what is behind and around you.

If arthritis is an issue, bigger knobs and easy to hit buttons can help. Also consider a larger diameter steering wheel that does not require you to close your hands so tightly. And a larger stick shift can be easier to manage.

Technology brings to play some features that can make driving safer and a bit more James Bond like. Small screens in the center of the console give you an unobstructed view of what is behind as you back up. Alarms are available that beep if something is in your path as you back up and beep faster as you get closer. Easy-fill tire alert systems allow you to pump air into your tires and when they reach the right inflation, the car horn chirps to notify you. Remote control door and trunk openers are easier to handle than the old key in the lock we grew up with. There is even a SUV that allows you to open the hatch by a simple kicking motion under the rear bumper assuming your hands may be full but your feet are generally available. And leave it to Mercedes-Benz to develop fatigue monitoring systems that help detect when a driver is in danger of falling asleep at the wheel. What will they think of next?

Technology has stepped up once again to make our lives easier. But it can only go so far. In the end these improvements may help extend the driving career of some senior citizens. But it is important to remain as objective as possible when evaluating your real ability to drive. No one but you knows if you are truly capable of driving safely. If the time should come that you know in your heart it is not safe for you to drive, do the right thing and surrender your keys.

Chapter 11 - Living to be 100

It is not by the gray of the hair that one knows the age of the heart.
~ Edward Bulwer-Lytton

Do you want to live to be one hundred years old? Such a question would have given rise to a scoffing chuckle not so very long ago. Back at the turn of the century the average life expectancy was less than fifty. And yet today a variety of factors have combined to add to our potential longevity from advances in medical care to improvements in nutrition to support networks and communities where like-aged individuals can live and engage in extended quality lives. It is no longer so far-fetched to hope to break that triple-digit age marker. According to the Census Bureau there were 53,364 centenarians alive as of December 2010.(6) If we fast forward to 2050 this number is projected to balloon to more than 600,000.(7) Assuming each of these individuals retired at age sixty five, they would experience thirty five years of retired life and all it has to offer.

However, such extended lifetimes may prove to be a mixed blessing as additional years will require additional resources. Beyond the significant increase in financial requirements to live to ripe old age, this aging population will face non-financial challenges providing a fulfilling and engaging retirement that takes into consideration their advanced years. As I have shared one of my biggest retirement fears is running out of worthwhile ways to spend my time in retirement. Adding more years can make this even more challenging. On the other hand if I discover those passions that drive me and excite me and make each day worth living, additional years may make things even better.

"How old are you? Well, I don't buy green bananas!" ~ Quick response from 89 year old woman still going strong.

Living to one hundred could be the adventure of a lifetime but only provided we are able to enjoy the journey. Assuming we will remain relatively healthy during our bonus years, both physically and mentally, it is exciting and somewhat mind boggling to think how much more productive each life could be. Additional years of learning and experience could mold us all into more well-rounded individuals. With more years to focus on areas where we need to improve, we might do away with some of those bad habits that have plagued us. And with more time we can do more of what we like to do. On the other hand if we are physically challenged or mentally unable to appreciate the life we live, a long life can be a lonely, painful excursion. It is all about the quality of life lived rather than the quantity of years.

Starting back in 2006, United Healthcare began surveying centenarians to raise awareness to keys to living a long and healthy life. Their *100@100 Survey* shared some interesting findings. (8)

- 35 percent of centenarians surveyed felt they owed their long life to a healthy lifestyle which included getting plenty of sleep, eating a healthy diet, limiting consumption of alcohol and not smoking. There are no real surprises here but rather a reinforcement of the basic secrets to living a long life we have known all along. As obvious as this prescription may be it does offer a useful starting point from which to shape our individual lifestyle as we endeavor to launch our long life.

- The latest technology is not necessarily the secret to a longer life – 44 percent said that the electric refrigerator was the technological innovation that had the most impact on their life. As for high tech, not so much – only 13 percent have access to the internet, 6 percent use email, and none have ever used Twitter. Technological advancements can make our lives a bit easier, perhaps a tad more efficient, and definitely more comfortable. But at least according to this study they are not necessarily the fountain of youth some may have hoped for.

People are living longer, much longer. I've found that many retirement plans project through to 90 at the oldest. But what if you live to 100? What about longer? Our ideas about retirement may need to dramatically change, especially if we see continued improvements in healthcare.

When I think what it would be like to live to 100 I experience mixed feelings. On the positive side of things I am living longer – there is nothing wrong with that. Life is wonderful and the world a beautiful playground made up of unique and interesting people and places. More years gives us more time to get out there and experience.

What worries me is the real possibility that while I might be continuing on toward my triple digit target, many around me would not be so fortunate. Since living to such an old age is the exception rather than the rule, it is likely that I would outlive some if not all of those I love. The prospect of spending many years without my spouse to share the moments frightens and saddens me. I cannot imagine outliving my children but that would be a real possibility. If my reward for living those many years is to outlive those most important to me and I will face a loneliness that can carry on for years, I don't think I really want to live to 100.

And then there is the whole loss of independence that surely must occur along a path toward becoming a centenarian. Let's face it we do not very often see a lot of healthy looking free-wheeling folks pushing 100. And despite whatever medical and technical advancements might come along that is probably the way it will remain. Our bodies are only good for so long and over time they wear out. And 100 years is a long time. In my mid-fifties now already beginning to feel the toll of time on knees and joints I have a hard time picturing what it will be like in another 45 years.

If we do happen to live onward and eventually approach age 100 that life we live will be quite different than what we are accustomed to. We will be forced to deal with changes and challenges every step of the way. Our dependence on others will grow and we will need to learn to embrace the reality of the person we are becoming. But we are here, still alive and kicking, and we need to make the best of it. In the end, it is up to each of us to do what we can to positively influence the quality of the life we will live. If we can get it right, if we are fortunate to experience a quality life on toward 100, it might just be a wonderful thing. As the Guatemalan proverb says, *"Everyone is the age of their hearts."*

While we may dream of living to a triple-digit age, it can be helpful to keep our feet on the ground and face a few facts. We need to focus on what is under our control and we want to be realistic in our expectations. There is nothing we can do to change the genes we are born with. Like it or not chances are very good that we will someday closely resemble our mother or father or more likely a little bit of both. The good the bad and the ugly of how we will look and behave further down the road can be clearly previewed each time we gaze upon our parents. And along with the physical appearance we can count on similarities in other areas. Little things like the particular way a phrase is turned or a familiar lilt to a laugh, perhaps a sense of humor that is truly a chip off the old block, sometimes a walk or mannerism that is so familiar we are on occasion mistaken for one another.

In addition to appearance, your health and susceptibility to certain ailments is in large part predetermined by your family. Exercise and diet and lifestyle choices all play a part in living a healthy life. But no matter what you do, you cannot escape your genes. That said, if you have a family history of heart disease or cancer or any of the other myriad of diseases that increase your likelihood of contracting the same, it is wise to see your physician on a regular basis. You cannot change your genetic makeup but ignoring it is not a good idea. Accept the reality that you are at risk and stay on top of it. There are things you can do and medicines you can take to preemptively address trouble areas. You can't fight Mother Nature but you can give her a run for her money by facing the facts and taking appropriate action.

The second thing we should do for our own sanity is attempt to set realistic expectations. It is generally safe to say that if we are willing to work hard and do the things required to live a healthy lifestyle, we can hope to realize improvements and experience positive results. However, we will not necessarily achieve the pinnacle of perfection that we are so often exposed to on TV and modern media. No matter how hard I workout it is not likely that I will ever replicate that seventy year old guy with the twenty inch biceps and washboard abs prominently displayed on nationwide ads. And despite our best efforts chances are slim that we will too closely resemble those older actors and actresses who so proudly grace the big screen. After all they have a squad of makeup magicians and personal trainers and must work extremely hard to maintain their ever-fleeting illusion of perfection. Yes we can positively impact our personal health in ways that will allow us to more fully enjoy life and retirement living. But we want to remember to be realistic. It can be discouraging to set impossible goals and unrealistic expectations since the likelihood of their achievement is small.

So do you really want to live to be 100? You would be in a small minority but you could possibly live that long.

Thoreau said, *"None are so old as those who have outlived enthusiasm."*

In the final analysis what it really comes down to is not necessarily the quantity of life as much as the quality of life. Yes more years sounds good but only if during those years we are reasonably aware, engaged, and able to live as close to normal a life as possible. Although as we age we learn to reluctantly accept our diminishing capacities we need to sustain that fire inside, that individual spark that makes us who we are. Few of us would likely opt to live just for the sake of being alive. And we don't want to choose to merely exist. If we are blessed to live to one hundred our feeling of thankfulness will depend in part upon the quality of life we are living. And if it is truly a quality life may the ranks swell with happy centenarians.

Chapter 12 - Don't Save It All for Retirement

We are always getting ready to live but never living. ~ Ralph Waldo Emerson

The plan for how my life was going to be was relatively clear from my early days. First, get a good education while attempting to figure out an appropriate career to pursue. Next, work in said career for a bunch of years during which time I raise my family while simultaneously building my savings and investments and in a perfect world paying down the mortgage on the house. Finally, once I have a sufficient nest egg to allow me to depart the working world, I step boldly into that happy carefree stage of life otherwise known as retirement. I did not have a hard and fast target retirement age but 65 seemed reasonable. It all made perfect sense when I was younger and continued to be the path I followed reasonably closely throughout my working years.

During those working years I accepted the reality that I would have to do without some things now if I planned to have what I would need to live comfortably from age 65 onward. Trips I would have loved to take were put on the back burner as they were too expensive. Impressive fancy houses remained a dream replaced by smaller more realistic dwellings that met the basic requirements of family and budget. Sexy sleek sport cars were something I looked at enviously from the seat of the same car I drove for thirteen years and 200,000 miles. But I accepted my fate and tightened my belt and fought the good fight.

The view of that perfect retirement life where money would not be such an issue and free time would be in abundance kept me going. I have generally been cool with the idea of paying your dues first before you reap your just rewards. Study first then play. Get your workout done and then have a beer. Make your allotted number of phone calls before you allow yourself to go to lunch. Say no to that new toy so you can save the money. Sacrifice now so you can enjoy later. I did on occasion splurge, but the driving theme was one of living frugally.

But I am beginning to realize that when it comes to putting off now what you hope to have the time and money to experience when you retire might not always be the best course of action. It might not be the best idea to save everything until after you retire.

You could be worn out by 65
A reader of my blog shared her perspective on the real challenges to be faced with life after 65. In our discussion about the possibility of working in some capacity after retirement she explained that "a lot of us are worn out by 65". She continued to describe how "retirement is very difficult" after having worked more than 25 years at a job that she enjoyed with the same people she knew and

loved and hated to leave behind. Contrary to some beliefs that retirement is the place to be, she says "there is nothing like being young or middle aged and being part of an organization we love." She enjoyed what she was doing and the people she worked with.

Then age 65 rolled around and she was forced to retire. What she quickly realized was that retirement living took a lot of effort. While on the job her days were busy and active. She was an object in motion and tended to remain in motion with momentum carrying her forward. Shift to retirement and suddenly she is tasked with filling her day with activities and events. It became challenging to find worthwhile and engaging things to fill the days and months. And at the core of it all was the fact that she was tired. Even though her career did not require extreme physical exertion, after 25 years at the same old grind she was worn out.

There was so much more that she wanted to do, so many adventures she had yet to live but the energy required sometimes seemed more than she could muster. She began to second guess herself and all of the careful saving and sacrificing that defined her pre-retirement life. She had put off so much at a time in her life when she was more physically able to enjoy the experience. Now those same little excursions might require more resources than she is able to call upon. Had she missed the boat?

We read inspiring stories about elderly people still living the life of someone half their age. Sixty year olds who are swimming for miles in chilly ocean waters or seventy year olds who are climbing impressive mountain peaks or eighty year olds who are writing novels. Each makes us smile and take notice but we tend to view these as the exceptions. The majority of those in advanced age groups tend to be far from adventurous typically more focused on getting by rather than flying high. By the time they reach age 65, many can be physically and mentally used up. Manufacturing jobs with their endless repetition requiring taxing physical effort can take a lasting toll after a long career. Even the knowledge workers of today who may not be physically worn out can easily find themselves exhausted from the constant stress that is part of their normal job. When 65 rolls around and you have time to do what you want it may turn out all you really want is to take a break.

Rather than delay experiencing all of your dreams and adventures until after you retire you might want to sample the menu a bit and enjoy a few courses along the way. Although it can be inspiring to climb Mt Rainier at age 65 it can be quite an enjoyable experience to do the same twenty years earlier when it is more of an everyday occurrence than a newsworthy event.

Try not to save all of your dream adventures and experiences for retirement when you may find yourself too old to enjoy their full potential. On the other hand do your best to be reasonable and don't spend your entire life savings doing everything you want before you reach age 65 either. A little balance can go a long way.

Hit the road while the hitting is good

Build a budget that allows you to separate living expenses from LIVING expenses. Then start planning your next LIVING experience the minute you get home from your last trip! Plan on one big fling each year and plan it to the hilt. Go to Honduras and lie on the beach or traverse through the canopy of a triple canopy jungle. Retire outside your comfort zone.

My parents have traveled the world widely over their 57 years together. In the early days while just starting their family they lived in Germany. On weekends and days off they drove hither and yon to thoroughly explore the Western European countries. Their slide collection of places visited is world class. And at their young age travel was exciting rather than taxing. They could not wait to hit the road and see what lay beyond the next turn.

Recently they have come to the decision that they will make no more long distance flights. The hassle of air travel has increased at the same time their tolerance levels have diminished. These days it is just too much for them to lug two suitcases plus two carryon bags through the huge international airports through ticket lines and security lines and baggage claims. And sitting in a plane wedged in a coach seat for ten hours only makes things worse.

But they did the right thing by traveling while they were younger. They had the opportunity and took advantage of it and have many wonderful memories. Understand that when mom and dad travel they are not looking for top of the line accommodations. They are frugal travelers who know a good deal and will search until they find said deal. With this attitude of doing it affordably they did not negatively impact their long term savings efforts. And they visited some of the most beautiful and world famous spots on the globe at a time when they were energetic, excited and nimble as mountain goats.

Travel after age 65 is not quite like travel at age 45. A younger you can be willing and able to walk those extra miles to visit that special spot off the beaten path. A younger you can stay up into the late hours to witness the music and night life of your destination and be no worse for the wear the next morning. A younger you is better equipped to roll with the inconveniences and unexpected hassles that travel inevitably involves and instead focus on the good things. It can be a mistake to put off traveling to all your dream locations until after you retire. Save a few sure, but if possible take advantage of the younger you to explore the world around while knees are sound, hearts are strong, and energy knows few bounds.

Take advantage of the best health you will likely have

Jonathan Swift said, *"Every man desires to live long, but no man would be old."* We hope for a long, healthy and happy life with sufficient time to enjoy and appreciate the many people, places and things that make up our universe. As is the case with many the busy nature of life sometimes delays our efforts to experience it all. But the promise of free time and free choice when we retire can help us hold our chin high and fly our optimism at full staff. There is light at the end of the tunnel – we just have to get there in one piece.

Sadly when we are finally ready to begin our retirement regimen we may encounter a less than perfect landing. Out of the blue we may discover those simple things we used to do are requiring a bit more effort these days. It is just not as easy as it used to be. We can find ourselves expending more effort to accomplish what at an earlier age was a breeze. It may be the case that the good health taken for granted while we were young is sadly nowhere to be found. And the reality is it is not likely to get any easier.

It can be a gamble to forego entirely today with the hope you can do tomorrow. When tomorrow comes you may not be the same person you are today. You do not know that you will be capable of doing those things you delayed. You cannot foresee the degree to which every day undertakings might become challenging. You do not even know that tomorrow will come. What a sad state of affairs to have all the time in the world but lack the ability to pursue your dreams.

If possible try not to save everything for retirement. While you are healthy today – likely as healthy as you will ever be – take advantage and get out there. Don't wait, do it now.

If we wait until we finally retire before we pursue our passions and sample our dreams we may find we have missed the boat, the window of opportunity has closed, that dog don't hunt. Despite the abundant availability of time we may find we just don't have the energy or ability.

Don't put your passions on hold

The thing that inspires me most is figuring out ways to go above and beyond for others. It's so easy to trudge through life without making an impact on others. So many times we are too busy with our own bills, chores and responsibilities that when someone goes out of their way for you, it is truly remarkable. My best weeks are the ones where I get to do a little extra something. It makes life feel less like a hamster on a wheel and more like life has some meaning.

I have raised two wonderful children who are on their respective paths to living what we all hope to be happy and fulfilling lives. I am excited about the wonderful opportunities that await them as they explore and experiment with all that life has to offer. I am optimistic of the outcome, I am enjoying living vicariously with them along their journey, and of course I am bit nervous as we do not know for sure what the future holds. And I hope that my constant nagging and preaching that they will be happiest if their career and life is spent doing what they love sticks with them.

If I could recommend one thing for my kids and other kids and just plain people in general it would be to do all you can as early in life as possible to find what it is that you are most passionate about. Harriet Tubman said, *"Always remember, you have within you the strength, the patience, and the passion to reach for the stars to change the world."* Try to figure out what it is that you want from your life, what it is that you want to be doing with your life and bottom line what it is that you really love. Your passion is not always apparent and can be difficult to decipher. Even when you are fortunate enough to come face to face with what really inspires it may very well change over the course of your life. But imagine a life where each day you awake to a clear picture of what most turns you on about living and your job is to do just that. Try to picture a job that you actually enjoy where you are engaged in doing what matters to you and what you love. Or take a peek down the road at a retirement where you have no time to contemplate boredom as you busily pursue avenues that stimulate and engage your intellect and heart.

I realize that most reading this book are further along in your lives than my children. Whether or not you were able to pursue your life's passion during your years of family raising and work, you are here now. Would you believe me if I told you it is not too late? There is still time to find what you are passionate about and do it. If you really want to spend your time doing what you like most, you still have a chance to discover exactly what that is. But do not wait for the quite hours of retirement living before you begin. Get started on your search today. Start living a life that is worthwhile, inspiring, exciting, and fun. Experiment, try new things but try something. Don't wait for your passion to find you as each day wasted is gone forever.

Try to experience your passions throughout your life. And just imagine how much better your transition into retirement when the activities you choose to fill your days are on those things that most inspire and excite you.

Baby boomers and anyone planning retirement or recently retired should realize that emotional planning is important too. Going from a full time job to no job may seem ideal, but it is an enormous and difficult adjustment. Many retired people end up feeling useless, with no purpose. They suffer from periodic depression as a result, making what could be the best time of their lives the worst time. Prepare yourself by finding a passion to pursue in retirement.

Chapter 13 - What will be your Legacy?

I want it said of me by those who knew me best
that I always plucked a thistle and planted a flower
where I thought a flower would grow.
~ Abraham Lincoln

How do you want to be remembered? Fifty years from now when your children and grandchildren are sitting around a fire sharing a fond memory, what would you hope they would say about you and the life you lived? Would their memory include that particular thing about which you were most proud, your greatest achievement? Or is it possible that they do not even know what that special something was? And how important is to you whether they do or don't?

For some, their legacy is a very important consideration. In extreme cases what is left for posterity is even more important than the individual life lived. Building a dynasty for future generations has driven more than one successful family to dizzying heights of fame and fortune. The entire focus of one's life becomes adding in some way to the family, improving their name, standing and revered place in history.

For those with less lofty aspirations, the importance of leaving a legacy can vary. I have spoken with people who plan on living their life to the fullest up to the last possible moment, not concerned with saving for future generations. Whatever might remain when they are gone is not an issue. What is important is enjoying life with whatever resources are at their disposal. Having established a life for themselves they expect their children to be capable of doing the same.

Others want to share the rewards of their labors and their successes with the next generation, perhaps giving them a bit of a head start on the future. Some leave behind money or property or whatever in hopes of providing a safety net for children should a challenge arise down the road. There are those who may wish to provide resources that can serve as a launch point for future generations to pursue their dreams or take a shot at a career that they genuinely love. For some, life has been a difficult struggle every step of the way and only through perseverance and luck were they able to succeed. They do not want their children to have to go through the same challenges and therefore provide a stake in their future via some inheritance.

And then there are those who view leaving an inheritance as a potentially bad thing. Money given without any effort spent might spoil the recipient or cause them to feel entitled in life. Why work when I have all I need? If we make it too easy, they might squander their talents and waste their lives in pursuit of meaningless distractions. Of course if you are happy with giving your kids a permanent life of leisure that is your option.

Retirees do not owe their kids ANYTHING! For some reason, kids think otherwise. They want their "inheritances" and will scream bloody murder if any of what they expect is given to a non-family member or has been spent by the parents.

Is leaving a legacy important to you?

How do you want to be remembered? Are you there yet?

I believe it is human nature that we want others to think well of us. Much of our life is spent searching for acceptance and reinforcement of our individual worth. We are careful not to offend and try to respect others, ever hopeful of receiving similar treatment in return. A little praise can go a long way and we all want to ultimately be perceived as praiseworthy.

If I have done any deed worthy of remembrance, that deed will be my monument. If not, no monument can preserve my memory.
~ Agesilaus II

If it is important how you are remembered, one excellent course of action is to focus on who you are right now. It is the person and life you live today that will build future memories and become the substance of fireside stories to be told. If you want to be remembered as a loving caring person, do your best to live that role in your daily endeavors. If you want people to think back on your incredible wit and sense of humor, you better get them laughing today. And if you want to be remembered for your generosity, don't wait until your last will and testament to start sharing with others. Try to do the things today that you hope to be remembered for tomorrow.

If there are bad habits that you maintain or inappropriate anger that you display or uncaring actions you exhibit toward those around you, guess what you will most likely be remembered for? In retirement you can make good use of your free time by cleaning house and doing your best to rid yourself of negative attributes. Try to fine tune your personality into that person everyone wants to be around. That is one way to foster those fond memories to be.

Do what you can to clear the air of any lingering conflicts from times gone by. If there is friction between you and a family member, maybe you want to be the bigger person and take the first steps to make amends. My father and his brother had a falling out many years ago and I could tell from dad's perspective that it hurt. He missed his brother and the history they shared but over time the divide seemed to increase rather than narrow. Recently my dad made one final outreach via a heartfelt letter. When he heard back a week later the news could not have been better. Both brothers apologized for past things said and done in the heat of the moment. The lines of communication have been re-opened and I am sure both feel a thankful relief to have moved on. But someone has to take the first step. Will it be you? Wouldn't you prefer to be remembered as the caring individual who extended an olive branch in search of peace rather than that stubborn, strong-willed old cuss who believed he was infallible to the bitter end?

Try this – sit down with a piece of paper and pen in a quiet spot. Ask yourself, "How would I describe me?" and start writing. Be honest in your observations of the person you are today, the same person you will ultimately be remembered as. Don't focus on creating a literary work of art but rather brainstorm a bit and build your profile. Take your time, don't force it but put your thoughts to paper. When you are done and you have reviewed your words, there is one more question to ask: "Is this the person I want to be remembered as?"

What is it that you are most proud of?

Is there something that you have accomplished during your life that truly makes you proud? Is there a cause or organization that you championed because it was so worthy of support? Did you in some way positively impact the life of another that still leaves you feeling good inside? All of these are clear indicators of the person you are and the passions you feel. If being remembered for the person you really are is important, you should share these moments and experiences with those around you.

What will you leave behind?

A legacy is often about leaving behind something of financial worth. Whether investments, a house, a car, or a trust fund, the focus is on dollars and cents. We discussed earlier leaving a legacy that reflects the person you were and the good you did while alive. And we touched on the idea that you can influence the memory others will have by living a quality, loving, meaningful life worthy of future adoration and fondness.

What is it you most want to share with future generations?

Is there an important story that you want to tell? If so, take the time to record it while it is fresh in your mind.

Do you want to record the family history for future generations? If so, get started on that family tree, start sorting through the boxes of pictures that have accumulated, and start documenting those unique stories that make up the history of your family.

And if the most important legacy is the memory of the person you were, do what you can to become that truly memorable person now.

My dad has been many things to me over the years. He has taught me the importance of being honest in dealings with others and having a clear conscience when you go to bed at night. He has ingrained in me the appreciation of beauty in nature from the majestic sunsets to the gentle babbling brook, from the dazzling display of wild flowers that bloom each spring in the Sierra Foothills to the incredible deep blue of Lake Tahoe. I have learned from him that there is truly beauty to be discovered in all people, places and things. Dad's attentions developed in me a love of music from the early days when he dragged this reluctant eight-year-old to hear the local symphony to the memorable barber shop quartet competitions we witnessed that still brings a smile to my face. But if there is one thing I most associate with dad it is his love and passion for fishing.

As a youngster he dragged me out of my warm bed in the early morning hours to sit in a little twelve foot aluminum boat that meandered along the San Joaquin Delta in search of Striped Bass. And I loved it. Later when he became a fly fisherman, we fished together in well equipped inner tubes floating on some of the most beautiful jewel-like lakes in the Eastern Sierra in search of native trout. And I loved it. But best of all was one little spot – Elephant Rock Lake – a tiny lake ringed by trees that you could walk around in about fifteen minutes. And within that lake were the most beautiful and lively Brook Trout you have ever seen. The best time to catch them was at dusk when you waded out about twenty feet from shore in water that was mid-thigh deep. All around the fish would be rising to catch insects, leaving behind ever-expanding rings on the surface as they quickly ducked down with their prize in mouth. It was a beautiful experience, a memorable moment and just the best time ever. I will always remember my dad as the ultimate fisherman who did not do it only to catch fish, but also because the places fish hang out tend to be some of the most beautiful on earth. Thank you dad for sharing your fishing legacy that has become a part of me.

When it comes down to it, whether you plan to or not, you will leave a legacy of sorts. The memories of you and the life you lived, your interactions with family and friends, your passions and dreams, and the unique quirks that make you who you are will be long remembered. You will have impacted a segment of the population for better or worse.

If it is material things for which you wish to be remembered, it is a simple matter of saving enough to procure said things. But beyond the things you leave behind, you will also leave a bit of you and who you were in all those who love you.

If I should die, said I to myself, I have left no immortal work behind me - nothing to make my friends proud of my memory - but I have loved the principle of beauty in all things, and if I had had

time I would have made myself remembered. ~
John Keats

Chapter 14 - The Retirement Holy Grail

Everything happens to everybody sooner or later if there is time enough.
~ George Bernard Shaw

Over the past years I have been gathering information and learning what I can to help better navigate the confusing retirement jungle out there. My goal is to find a way to eventually live a fulfilling worthwhile retirement. I have come to accept the fact that I am the kind of person who feels more secure knowing as much as possible about what is ahead. Obviously you cannot know everything and even a well-prepared plan is subject to unexpected events beyond our control. But that does not mean we cannot use the resources at our disposal, the experiences of those who have gone before us, and the brains we were born with to take our best shot. Even if we cannot foresee everything that will happen, I believe we can make some educated guesses and take actions to increase our odds of realizing that ideal retirement we read about in fairy tales. The trick is to know what you need to do and then get to it sooner rather than later.

I have spoken with many retirees as well as retirees to be to get their thoughts on what works and what does not. Since no one is an expert at retirement until they actually begin to live the experience, there is a lot of trial and error along the way. Sometimes retirement turns out to be exactly what was expected. Sometime retirees are surprised by unforeseen realities and the various challenges they face. I believe most of us will fall somewhere in between these two.

Some part of me wishes that I could be like other retirees that seem content to slow down and focus on families and hobbies, but I'm quite happy to realize that many people – like me – don't find the "hobbies and travel" life fulfilling. I didn't particularly like travel when I was working and didn't take much time for hobbies either, so I don't know why it was a surprise that work was deeply fulfilling to me. I haven't found the right volunteering atmosphere either yet, but will continue to look for it. My dad is 90 and just retired (and it's made him unhappy to do so even at his age). Maybe it's genetic.

I regularly follow numerous blogs and publications sifting through what the experts have to say on all matters retirement. As I said earlier, I find the information retirement-focused bloggers share to be incredibly valuable. They are generally at varying stages in the retirement process and share real life experiences that we can all learn from. Theirs is the life we will all one day live if we so choose. Their honest discussions and candid comments on the myriad of pieces making up the retirement planning puzzle can help to illuminate the sometimes murky waters we will soon find ourselves wading.

Since I have not retired yet, my perspective is based to a large extent on research that I am gathering along with insights and comments from those already retired. I have also taken time to seriously ask myself what does retirement means to me and how can I enjoy the experience rather than waste the moments. Since I have some years before I officially retire, what can I do between now and then to prepare? What can I learn from the experiences of those already retired to make better choices? What mistakes can I hope to avoid? What realities can I expect to encounter?

If I were to pick what I consider to be the top 10 most essential considerations as we prepare for our retirement the list would look like this:

(1) Be honest with yourself
No one knows what goes on inside your heart better than you. Those around you may learn to read signs and interpret moods to catch a glimpse of your inner motivations but at best they are only guessing. You have the power to deceive others by behaving in ways that are contrary to your true feelings such as smiling on the outside while you cry on the inside. But you cannot fool yourself.

We are all aging and the years ahead will bring a mix of good as well as bad. We can try to deny the effects of time but we will ultimately fail. We can make the best of what life throws our way but we must also be realistic. Victor Hugo said, *"When grace is joined with wrinkles, it is adorable. There is an unspeakable dawn in happy old age."*

Getting older will not be easy but it will be. Accepting reality and living the best life possible can earn you peace of mind at the end of the day. Don't try to kid yourself but rather face the day bravely, do the best you can to cope and be the best person you know you can be each day.

(2) Be easy on yourself as you transition into your new lifestyle

When starting out in retirement, try not to put unnecessary pressure on yourself right off the bat. Don't allow yourself to feel guilty if you find you have nothing to do. Try to accept that time you enjoy wasting is in fact not wasted at all. Learn to go with the flow and appreciate your good fortune at being retired. Allow yourself to settle into the new life you will be living. You have earned your freedom from responsibility so savor the moment.

The time may come when you want to explore more meaningful activities to fill your day. But you will be happier if you wait and see rather than jump immediately into something that you may quickly discover you would really rather not be doing.

You know I have been retired for 15 years. During the last 6 years I have done a lot of introspection and have decided that retirement is not brain surgery. It is simply another stage in our life. We continue to do pretty much the same things we have always done with one exception – we do them when and how we want.

(3) Live your legacy

Older people frequently talk about what they will leave behind when they are gone. Everyone wants to be remembered and our personal legacy is important, more so as we get on in years. For some it is all about leaving an estate or material goods so the next generation can benefit from the hard work and success realized during their life. Others are more concerned with how the life they lived and the person they were will be remembered.

Why not focus your efforts on the life you are living now to create a lasting memory that goes beyond material things? Long after your inheritance is spent the memory of who you were and what you stood for can live on. I would rather have my children or grandchildren remember my crazy sense of humor or my obsession with the San Jose Sharks hockey team or a kind deed I did for someone in need rather than line their pockets with money soon to be gone. If after I am gone they smile when they think of me, my legacy will live on.

(4) Don't be afraid to step outside of your comfort zone

By this time in life you are well aware of what makes you comfortable, what you like to do. You have probably been doing it for years and let's face it you have gotten darn good at doing it. Why shake things up? Why mess with a good thing? Because there can be even better things to be experienced if you are willing to step outside your comfort zone.

Do you remember while growing up when you did something for the very first time? The first time you rode your bike without training wheels while mom watched pensively from the porch. The first time you scored a run or a goal or a basket under the watchful eyes of happy teammates. The first award received for performance above the call of duty at school or work. Your first dance when you had no idea what you were doing but got out there on the floor nonetheless. Each of these memorable moments was the result of your willingness to take a chance, to try something new. There is no reason why we should unduly limit ourselves just because we are getting older. Life is meant to be lived and a little variety can spice things up nicely. What is comfortable is well known and familiar and safe. But what is exciting often requires a little something out of the ordinary.

"I see my path but I don't know where it leads. Not knowing where I'm going is what inspires me to travel it." ~ Rosalia de Castro

(5) Try to live below your means

Living a fulfilling retirement life does not require that you pursue extravagance. The good things in life may not all be free but spending more money does not guarantee they will be better. Frugality is a healthy state of mind not only in retirement but throughout our lives. The world is filled with uncertainty and there is no guarantee we will have tomorrow what we do today. As the years progress, we can hope to be that much more secure in our future with a bank balance that is at least to some extent under our control.

(6) Do not be a watcher, be a doer

TV is for watching. Sports events are for watching. Concerts are for watching. Theater is for watching. Life is for living.

A retirement life spent on the sidelines watching the world go by might be perceived by some as a retirement wasted. What can I do to get involved and engaged with living?

What I can try to do is live a healthy life including watching my diet and exercising regularly so the body I inhabit has the best chance to keep at it.

What I can do is try new things that I have not done before. If I do not like them I stop doing them. If I do like them I have discovered a new avenue to keep me moving.

What I can do is just do something, anything, rather than observe passively from the sidelines. I would prefer to have others watch what I am doing while I am busily engaged with living the moment. As Sydney Smith said, *"Regret for the things we did can be tempered by time; it is regret for the things we did not do that is inconsolable."*

(7) Do it now

The procrastinator puts off today what he can do tomorrow. Why hurry, why rush, what is the big deal? But the clock is ticking and no one knows how many more tomorrows we are allotted. Today is a great day to get it done. Now is the perfect time to try it, to do it, to live it.

I think we need a purpose in our retirement years and as we enter the second half of life, we actually have the time and inclination to pursue the idea of what makes us happy. What is really important? I think as we get older the answer to that question changes. Money is nice but to pursue your passion and purpose in life, you don't necessarily need money or to be hooked on the idea that you must make money from your passions. At our age, we should just be able to do what we want to do because we want to do it and for no other reason!

(8) Have no regrets

"A man is not old until his regrets take the place of his dreams." ~ Yiddish Proverb.

You know the story of the old guy on his death bed listing all of the things he is sorry for not having done during his life. Tears are shed as he describes spending too much time on the job, spending too little time with family, not going on that adventure he always dreamed of, not saying I love you to important family and friends over the years. No one wants to find them self in that place. But how many of us are taking action to prevent such an occurrence in our own lives?

Through our life we make mistakes, we forget to say things we should, we miss an opportunity to do good. These mistakes can haunt our retirement, leaving us with feelings of guilt and sorrow. Rather than accept the situation why not take this time to make amends, clear the air, and do the right thing.

My 24 year old son makes it a point to never head out the door before saying I love you. My wife and I never go to sleep at night before saying we love each other. We also have a pact that we will not go to bed angry. You never know if tomorrow will come.

(9) Don't let your passions die with you

So you are retired. You have time to do what you want. While you were tied up in the working world, you may have dreamed of just this chance to do what you really want, what inspires you and really excites you. Now that you are retired, are you doing it? Are you pursuing that passion that has been within you for only you know how long? If you are not, what are you waiting for?

Now can be the perfect time to do what you have always dreamed of doing. While you are still able, while you are still excited, while you have the time you need, do it. Don't ignore your passions when you finally have exactly what you need to bring them to life.

Time and choice are two of the biggest perks in retirement. To come to a full stop in life is to come to the end of the road. One of the problems of finding what one wants to do in retirement is when there is no passion for life before retirement, thus no areas to really spend those gifts of time and choice.

(10) Family First

What greater thing is there for human souls than to feel that they are joined for life – to be with each other in silent unspeakable memories.
~ George Elliot

My mom taught us all from an early age that there is nothing more important than family. No matter what life throws your way, you can always count on your family to be there for you, stand up for you and love you despite any and all faults. Although there may be times when disputes arise, there is no escaping the ties that bind.

Once we retire, our busy calendars may have a bit more time available to spend with others. And who better to spend that time with than family. If you are lucky to have your parents still around, call them and visit them and share your life's events. No one is prouder of you than mom and dad and no one wants more to be included in your life. If you have not spoken with a sibling recently, pick up the phone. Catch up with each other, share a memory and reconnect. If the last time you spoke ended in a conflict, mend that bridge and move on. Don't take for granted what many are jealous of – namely a family that cares and shares and loves.

Notes

(1) Retirement Confidence Survey- Preparing for Retirement in America, (2011) http://www.ebri.org/pdf/surveys/rcs/2011/FS2_RCS11_Prepare_FINAL1.pdf

(2) Oregon State University, Michelle Barnhart, Assistant Professor of Marketing, http://oregonstate.edu/ua/ncs/archives/2012/nov/study-examines-how-elderly-go-being-perceived-capable-consumer-%E2%80%98old-person%E2%80%99 (April 2013)

(3) Society of Actuaries Report, *The 2011 Risks and Process of Retirement Survey*, http://www.soa.org/files/research/projects/research-key-finding-longevity.pdf

(4) Social Security Administration, *When to Start Receiving Retirement Benefits*, http://www.socialsecurity.gov/pubs/10147.html#a0=1 , (August 2012)

(5) United States Government Accountability Office, *UNEMPLOYED OLDER WORKERS - Many face long-term joblessness and reduced job security*,

http://www.gao.gov/assets/600/590882.pdf, page 5, (May 15, 2012)

(6) US Census Bureau, *Centenarians: 2010,* https://www.census.gov/prod/cen2010/reports/c2010sr-03.pdf , (December 2012)

(7), (8) United Healthcare, *100@100 Survey,* http://www.unitedhealthgroup.com/news/rel2011/UHC-100at100-Results-Report.pdf , (November 2011)

About the Author

Dave Bernard is a California born and raised author and blogger with an extensive 30 year career in the Silicon Valley. Although not yet retired, he focuses on identifying and understanding those most essential considerations we will each need to address if we hope to realize a fulfilling and meaningful retirement.

He has written more than 300 blogs for US News & World *On Retirement* and his personal blog *Retirement – Only the Beginning.*

Candid feedback and thousands of comments from readers has given him a unique glimpse into the realities and challenges that all retirees will ultimately face, inspiring his most recent work *I Want To Retire! - Essential Considerations for the Retiree to Be.*

His other works include *Are you Just Existing and Calling it a Life* and a free e-book entitled *Navigating the Retirement Jungle.*

Dave lives in sunny California with his wife, two cats, and a passion for the San Jose Sharks hockey team.

He can be contacted at
LoveBeingRetired@hotmail.com

Connect with me online:

Twitter: http://twitter.com/djbernard

Facebook:
http://facebook.com/david.bernard.3998

Made in the USA
Monee, IL
06 November 2019